Making Rain and Other Things Is Our Business!

A. L. Smith

ISBN: 978-1-4834-0366-3 (sc)
ISBN: 978-1-4834-0368-7 (hc)
ISBN: 978-1-4834-0367-0 (e)

Library of Congress Control Number: 2013916914

Lulu Publishing Services rev. date: 09/25/2013

I dedicate this book to my long-suffering wife, Jean. Throughout the gestation period of this book, she has had to put up with, without putting too fine a word on it, me. She has long suspected that I was slightly mad; now she has the evidence.

I also dedicate this book to my daughters, Jayne and Hayley, and a Dutch girl, now a lady, called Patty, who made it all possible so many years ago in the Netherlands. Also to my granddaughters, Molly and Lauren, who have for some time harboured thoughts that I was odd; they will now be in a position to make an informed decision.

Finally, I wish to pay a special thanks to composer Lucy Pankhurst for her belief in my ability to write something that someone might be mad enough to read and that had the potential to lend itself to a musical portrayal. I hope she is right.

I have spent a considerable part of my life with my head in the clouds one way or another, and I just had to let it rain. You are on the receiving end. Have an umbrella handy!

CONTENTS

The Stories

Illustrations

Maps

PREFACE

Background to the Stories

In 1985 I took my wife, Jean, and my two daughters, Jayne (aged sixteen) and Hayley (aged eleven), on holiday to the Netherlands. I had rented a holiday home in a place called Hardewold in the province of Flevoland, just north of a town called Hardewijk. This was the first time I had driven a car on European roads, and it was something of a nervous challenge.

My daughters had been swimming in the holiday park pool, and when they returned to our holiday home, they brought with them a nine-year-old Dutch girl called Patricia Friedrichs, known to everyone as Patty. This bubbly Dutch girl amazed us by her fluency in the English language. Patty formed a friendship with my daughters and with Hayley in particular. Patty had never been taught English; she had picked it up by watching the British Forces TV network. She came from a town in the south of the country—Limburg province, to be precise—called Eygelshoven, which is close to the border with Germany.

Naturally we met Patty's parents, Lex and Ria, and formed a friendship that has lasted a very long time, although Lex sadly passed away some years ago. We learned from Patty about her school, the Veldhof School, and her teacher Mr Sonnemans. We also learned about some of her school friends, Rik Brouns, Iris Driessen, and Erica Eydems. She was a very lively and talkative young girl who went on to study at university in Amsterdam and is now a teacher herself.

In 1986 I visited the Friedrichs family whilst doing some work in Arnhem, and Lex introduced me to his town. Eygelshoven had been a Dutch coal mining town, and Lex had worked in the pay office in one of the local mines, but all that had come to an end. The mines had gone, but several pieces of mining machinery had been restored and were dotted around the town as a reminder of local heritage. I also got to see the Veldhof School. I was made exceedingly welcome in the Friedrichs family home in Willem Alexanderstraat.

The friendship between our two families blossomed, and just for fun in 1987 I wrote a story for Patty called "Mr Sonnemans's Unusual Solution". Lex translated the script and gave it to the school, to be read out to the children.

I rather enjoyed my little foray into the literary world, and after being surprised by my own imagination, I decided to write another story following on from the theme established by the first; I called it "The Nimbus Springs a Leak". Both of these stories were written for children.

One of my enduring memories was created in 1987, when I arranged for Hayley to travel to the Friedrich family to spend some time in the Netherlands and then to return with Patty so that she could spend some time here in UK. Hayley was dispatched from Manchester Airport to Rotterdam with an airline escort, to be met at the other end by Patty and her parents. Several weeks later our two young, intrepid travellers arrived back in Manchester, and they were a sight to behold, walking through the airport reception area like two little princesses. It was a slightly less confident Patty travelling back with an escort a few weeks later. It was Patty's absence from Eygelshoven at this time that inspired my next story, "The Great Patty Famine", because I knew that this was the first time she had been outside of the Netherlands.

I spared the world from my literary incursions for another twenty-five years. For some unexplainable reason, I suffered a serious attack of imagination in 2012, probably brought on by the experience of listening to a brass band (they tend to create pictures in my head, but I am receiving treatment for it) and falling off the settee from my usual horizontal position; I then leapt to the computer and started writing. In truth this had really been inspired by the fact that, having enjoyed listening to brass bands so much, I got this desire to tell my stories with music. By good fortune when I approached Lucy Pankhurst, a very talented composer who is making a name for herself around the world, to compose something for me, she agreed. Having re-read the stories, I had an idea to create something with those same Dutch children in mind who would now be adults and hence tell a story written in a more adult fashion. The Queen's Diamond Jubilee Year formed the basis for this story, which is called "The Great Cloud Parade", and I am most fortunate that Lucy will be composing a piece of music to represent it. I finished this story in April 2012.

Having got the bug again, I decided to follow up "The Great Cloud Parade" with another story in the same vein, and I called it "Where Have All the Clouds Gone" after completing it in September 2012. So far I have been very fortunate that the authorities have not come to take me away!

Having become a prisoner of my own imagination, I have now completed thirteen stories, the first two in 1987 and the rest in 2012-2013, which collectively form a book titled *Making Rain and Other Things Is Our Business.*

Tony Smith
March 2, 2013

ACKNOWLEDGEMENTS

My first foray into the world of storytelling has been a long and laborious journey, and I could not have done it without the help of certain individuals. My neighbour Helen has been most helpful, putting me right on commas, speech marks, and general punctuation and spelling, and without her help I may never have been launched. My dear friend Eddie, with whom I have had the pleasure of sharing some exciting flying experiences, turned his design skills to the production of my Cloud Machine plans. Tuba player Matthew has been instrumental in guiding me through the printing and publishing world to get me airborne. Last but not least, a thank-you to Mark, who designed the front cover of the book in such an enticing manner. Thank you to all of you, but please remember that when you visit me, I don't like grapes!

INTRODUCTION

Weather is both a natural phenomena and man-made, but in the case of the latter it has long been a government secret that Manchester is the home of man-made manufactured weather.

Man-made weather is produced on demand by specially produced Cloud Machines that, in cloud forms of many alternative types, convey rain at different levels to wherever it is required. Lightning, thunder, snow, and a myriad other weather forms are also available on demand.

Manchester is the only place in the world where Cloud Machines are manufactured, and Black, Black & Blackemore's in deeper Salford is the specialist in this field. Cloud Machine owners are registered and certificated. Their machines have annual MOT tests to keep their "certificates of airworthiness" current, and they are operated in strict accordance with the *Cloud Machine Operators Rules of Operation Manual.*

Work available for Cloud Machine owners is always advertised in Wythenshawe Weather Centre, and agreements are made there. Cloud Machines not in use are normally kept in a hangar at the centre. There are many other weather centres around the world, but they generally only deal with natural weather.

The stories told have, as a central figure, Cloud Machine owner Captain Cirrus Cumulus and his faithful engineer, Percival White (generally known as Puffy), who crew the *Nimbus*.

The first two stories were written in 1987. The first describes how the *Nimbus* was engaged to solve a Dutch teacher's dilemma, whilst the second illustrates how Dutch engineers were able to come to the rescue of the *Nimbus* as it delivered rain to Apeldoorn.

The next eleven stories were written in 2012-2013, and the first of these, "The Great Cloud Parade", describes how a royal commandment was complied with to celebrate the Queen's Diamond Jubilee, but it did not go completely to plan. The stories that follow provide an insight into how a group of clandestine operators empty one of Britain's most iconic lakes and how it gets filled again, but not without generating another watery problem.

Search and rescue, fund raising, display work, and foreign aid all feature in the life of a Cloud Machine and its owner. Even a rest period could turn out to be full of interesting events. Fighting criminal cloud activity may be a bizarre-sounding activity, but it was all in a day's work for Captain Cumulus and the *Nimbus*.

The stories culminate with the "Great Shindig", in which a nostalgic return is made to a remote Scottish island and celebrated in a unique style.

MR SONNEMANS'S UNUSUAL SOLUTION

A Teacher's Dilemma

It was Wednesday morning, February 17, 1988, and in the Veldhof School in Eygelshoven, Mr Sonnemans was teaching a class of pupils. The students were taking a great deal of interest in his lesson, which concerned the weather in England. Whilst being delighted with their response, he was equally perplexed at his own inability to provide answers to some of the children's questions.

"Why are those clouds called Manchester Blacks?" asked Iris Driessen, pointing at one of the enlarged photographs.

"That's because they are made by machines from Manchester, which as you know, is in the north-west of England. That's where they specialise in manufacturing clouds," he replied.

"You mean they actually make clouds in England?" inquired Rik Brouns.

"That's right," replied Mr Sonnemans. "And what's more, many of these English clouds find their way over to Holland when the wind blows in the right direction."

A sigh of disbelief rang around the room as the pupils looked at their teacher in amazement.

"Does that mean that when the weather is good here, there's a strike on in England?" piped up Erica Eydems, the class joker.

Everyone laughed, including Mr Sonnemans, who quickly retorted, "No, that's when the wind is on strike!"

Willy Heunen had been dying to ask a question for ages, and now was his opportunity. "Where do Cumberland Greys and Westmorland Whites come from, sir?"

"Well, Willy, Cumberland Greys and Westmorland Whites are made by the same machines, using the finest-quality water available, and the

English are particularly proud of them. Westmorland Whites are not much good for rain and are mostly used for the decoration of summer blue skies."

Not all of the morning's questions were easy to deal with, however. *How can I possibly explain to the children what "raining cats and dogs" means in England—and for that matter, "pea soup fog"?* mused Mr Sonnemans. Try as he might, he could think of no sensible thing to say and resolved to discuss the matter with the other members of staff.

The Start of a Solution

"Listen, Hans, try getting in touch with Mr Dikkars at the Maastricht Meteorological Centre. I'm sure he could advise you," said one of Mr Sonnemans's fellow teachers during the coffee break.

In due course, Mr Dikkars was contacted, with the result that the pupils in the Veldhoff School would soon witness a most unusual solution to their teacher's dilemma.

Captain Cumulus and his faithful engineer, Puffy White, descended in their Cloud Machine called the *Nimbus* towards the Wythenshawe Weather Centre in the south of Manchester.

"Slow ahead, Puffy," shouted the captain.

Puffy set the controls appropriately, and the *Nimbus* touched down gently outside one of the Weather Centre's large hangars. The crew stepped out of the bullet-shaped fuselage and walked through the mist that surrounded it. Captain Cumulus emerged first and looked back at what could only be described as a cloud on the ground.

"That's a very good Cloud Machine!" said the captain to himself.

The two crewmembers entered the Weather Centre by a large door. A corridor led to a flight of stairs, and the crew ascended them and then proceeded along a further corridor before entering a large hall. Along the walls were many cards, each advertising some job or other to convey clouds to every corner of the world. There were other cloud-machine captains there, too, and each of them was intently studying the jobs on hand.

"Come on, Puffy, let's see if we can find something different for a change."

Puffy looked with disdain at his captain, because he had strong memories of what "something different for a change" could mean!

Captain Cumulus scanned the multitude of cards, and few appealed to him. He paused momentarily at one requesting the delivery of heavy rain to dampen a forest fire in Wales. Another that caught his eye involved the delivery of snow in Scotland for a holiday ski run. The majority of jobs, however, were routine and were not different in the sense that the captain meant. "There's not much here today," complained the disgruntled captain.

Puffy's heart began to sink.

They were coming to the final display board when the captain spied the words "An Educational Trip to Holland", written in large letters on a card half hidden by another. He took the card from the board and looked at it more closely. "Mmm, this is a journey to Eygelshoven, in the south of Holland."

Puffy could see a smile appearing on his captain's face and was well pleased.

They took the card to the station office, where it was processed in the usual way. The *Nimbus* was back in business.

Preparing to Travel

"Right, Puffy, let's get cracking. There's work to do."

From that moment onwards, the two men worked feverishly to prepare the *Nimbus* for its latest assignment. Everything on board was checked to ensure that it was in working order. They loaded several barrels of green powder. They paid a visit to the local animal home. Finally they sailed out over the Irish Sea to take on board some four million gallons of suitable water.

"Switch on the atomiser, Puffy," called Captain Cumulus. Puffy dutifully complied, and within an hour the equipment had atomised four million gallons of seawater and converted it into the cloud that now embraced the control centre of the *Nimbus.*

The captain issued further instructions to determine the size, shape, and colour that the *Nimbus* would become for its journey to Holland. Puffy carried out each one carefully, and at the end of it all they had created a dark-grey, bulbous cloud of voluminous proportions.

Puffy raised a periscope so that the captain could view his way forward. It was no ordinary periscope, because it contained a camera that produced the picture on the TV set placed just forward of the helm.

It was early evening, and the captain looked at his watch. At precisely 7:00 pm, he gave the instruction to start up the vessels motor and set it for half speed. The *Nimbus* swung through several degrees in response to the turning of the helm and came to rest when the captain observed the correct compass reading. The *Nimbus* was starting on her educational trip to Holland!

The Journey Begins

In the early part of the journey, the crew observed the twinkling lights of English towns below, but whilst the hurly-burly of life carried on down there, Captain Cumulus and Puffy sailed on in a silent night sky. The silence was broken only by the music of the wind as it first accelerated through small gaps between mountain-like clouds and then spent itself harmlessly in a black abyss. Adjacent clouds constantly changed their shape to present a wondrous cavalcade that delighted the captain.

They left the twinkling lights behind as the *Nimbus* began to cross the North Sea. With neither the coast of England nor Holland in view, the crew became aware of the total beauty of the night sky, with its myriad stars and, on this occasion, a full moon that ensured that each cloud had a silver aura. This was the silent world in which Captain Cumulus plied his business. He, too, was silent, because words were not needed to appreciate the tranquillity of this private panorama.

The hours passed, and eventually winking lights in the distance ahead heralded the Dutch coast.

"Dutch coast coming up!" cried Puffy.

The sound of Puffy's voice brought Captain Cumulus to the sudden realisation that he had been dreaming. "Keep her on the present course, Puffy," answered the captain, a little embarrassed at having been disturbed that way.

The *Nimbus* crossed the coast at Egmond-aan-Zee and continued to proceed in an eastwards direction.

"Shall I alter course, Captain?" asked Puffy.

"No; we stay on the present course until we reach Apeldoorn. We'll change then and not before then," replied the captain sternly.

Apeldoorn? thought Puffy, *That's miles out of our way. Why in heaven's name does the captain want to go via Apeldoorn?*

The *Nimbus* sailed serenely on in the night sky as the lights below began to go out one by one; people were retiring to their beds. By the time they reached Apeldoorn, few lights were on to indicate its presence.

The captain gave the order, "Slow ahead," and the *Nimbus* momentarily came to a halt. Captain Cumulus took a jug marked "Rob's Tea" from a shelf and took a long drink from it. He then placed the jug back on the shelf and placed his elbows on the table in front of him, resting his chin in the cups of his hands. For several minutes he appeared to be deep in thought and somewhat perplexed. "Right, Puffy, let's set course for Arnhem," barked a clearly agitated Captain Cumulus.

The faithful Puffy complied, as he always did.

During the journey south from Apeldoorn, several adjustments to the vessel's speed were necessary. Timing on this particular job was very important.

The *Nimbus* sailed over Arnhem, Nijmegen, Boxmeer, Venlo, Roermond, and Sittard, as dawn began to break. The people below could have no idea what was going on above their heads.

The Solution Is Delivered

By 9:00 am on Wednesday, February 24, the pupils in the Veldhof School in Eygelshoven were beginning their lessons. Mr Sonnemans was excited at the prospect of what was about to happen, and he anxiously peered at his watch several times.

The *Nimbus* was on schedule, and with speed at a minimum, she slowly sailed over Heerlen in the direction of their destination. At exactly 9:15 am Puffy emptied the barrels of green powder into a mixing machine whilst the captain studied his map of Eygelshoven most carefully. Slowly but surely, the *Nimbus* descended to one hundred feet.

"There is the marketplace, and the Laurastraat," cried the captain, looking at his TV monitor. "Let me see now," he murmured to himself.

"We proceed along the Veldhofstraat, then right into Anselderlaan, and the Veldhof School should be on the right."

"There it is, Captain, right below us," shouted Puffy, who had been watching over the captain's shoulder.

"Switch on the mixing machine, Puffy, and operate the luminance control. We are about to descend to ground level now." Captain Cumulus quickly glanced at his watch to check that they had arrived on time.

It was 10.00 am when the first pupils in Mr Sonnemans's class became aware of a green cast outside the classroom window. A green mist was slowly descending onto Veldhof School. Its presence was not unnoticed by the teacher, but he was determined not to be surprised by it. Rik Brouns and Danny Eygelshoven could not resist the temptation to speak and called Mr Sonnemans's attention to the green mist outside.

"A green mist? That's no ordinary green mist—that's English 'pea soup fog'," replied Mr Sonnemans.

The pupils were encouraged to walk to the windows and peer out into the green fog delivered from England.

"Can we go outside sir?" asked Nicole Jacobs.

"Of course, but you must all hold hands," was the reply.

Bert Gartener was puzzled by his teacher's instruction, but not for long. As soon as Bert entered the thick 'pea soup fog', he couldn't see his hand in front of his face.

The green fog was damp and cold, and the pupils soon came back into the classroom. Mr Sonnemans had a gleam in his eye when he said, "Well, children, that's what is known as 'pea soup fog' in England, and it has been specially delivered just for you to see."

The pupils were delighted and gave Mr Sonnemans a great cheer.

The *Nimbus* was shrinking to a dangerously small size, and the green fog condensed as it came into contact with the buildings of the Veldhof School and the ground. If this was allowed to continue, its secret would be revealed to all. However, there was a very special reason that this mission had been possible in the first place. On a small square of grass between the Andselderlaan and Wimmerstraat was a strange-looking machine that was orange in colour and made from old mining equipment. No one in Eygelshoven knew its purpose or whether it had one at all, but it was clearly marked on Captain Cumulus's map. It was a secret cloud pump.

"Okay, Puffy, let's move slightly east to the cloud pump," ordered the captain.

Puffy adjusted the throttle, and the *Nimbus* carefully and slowly moved until it was alongside the strange-looking orange machine.

The door of the *Nimbus* was opened and its access ladder deployed. Puffy stepped down into the green mist wearing a special visor to enable him to see. He pulled a large, plastic tube from the underside of the *Nimbus* and connected it to the open end of the cloud pump. Then he manipulated two large levers at the opposite end so that the *Nimbus* could be refuelled. The whole process was invisible to the townsfolk because of the density of the pea soup fog. Within five minutes the *Nimbus* was replenished and ascended to one hundred feet, returning to its normal grey colour at the same time in preparation for the next part of its job.

Only fifteen minutes had passed since the green fog had suddenly lifted from the Veldhof School. The class joker, Erica Eydems, shouted, "Mr Sonnemans, it's raining cats and dogs."

That was a signal for everyone to rush to the windows. Each face pressed up hard against the window panes and looked heavenward in amazement, because Erica was certainly correct—it was raining cats and dogs! Each small creature, suspended from a miniature parachute, slowly descended to the ground.

"Oh, Mr Sonnemans, they are so beautiful," remarked Willy.

"Who did this for you, Mr Sonnemans?" asked Iris.

"That must remain a secret," Mr Sonnemans replied.

Try as they might, the pupils couldn't get their teacher to reveal his secret, but there was one person in the class who could guess who it was!

Captain Cumulus was well pleased with the job he had done and took off his cap to wave good-bye to the Dutch people down below. He had a special place for them in his heart and could never resist an opportunity to visit their country. He wiped a tear from his eye as he set course for England.

"Okay, Puffy, now that that job is done, let's take a drink of Rob's tea!"

Puffy looked at his captain in amazement, because it was a rare privilege indeed to share the captain's drink.

"Here's to Mr Sonnemans's unusual solution," said the captain, raising his tea cup for a toast with Puffy. As they drank, Eygelshoven and the Veldhof School disappeared from view, but the image of the *Nimbus* still remains today inside many a Dutch head.

THE NIMBUS SPRINGS A LEAK

Another Dutch Job

Puffy White came racing up the gangplank of the *Nimbus,* which was anchored between jobs in one of the huge cloud hangars at the Wythenshawe Weather Centre. Captain Cumulus was busy polishing the brass work in the control room when Puffy burst in.

"We have a job over Holland, Captain," shouted Puffy excitedly.

The captain had friends in Holland and always looked forward to visiting the country. "Well, bless my soul!" he exclaimed. "Where are we headed?"

"Apeldoorn," replied Puffy.

"Whatever do we have to do there?" asked the captain.

"According to the instructions, we have to drop a load of Manchester Blacks!"

Manchester Blacks happened to be some of the finest clouds made in the north of England. Once airborne, they looked quite menacing, and upon sighting them, people would scatter in all directions in the expectation of a sudden downpour.

The *Nimbus* was fairly new, having been built some two years earlier in Black, Black & Blakemore's yard in deeper Salford. She was designed to carry up to four million gallons of water of all grades. When fully loaded, she was a "juggercloud" without any doubt. Captain Cumulus could, with the help of his controls, determine the size, shape, and colour of the *Nimbus,* which meant that he captained a very versatile Cloud Machine indeed.

"Right, Puffy, its Apeldoorn here we come, with a full load of Manchester Blacks. When do we have to deliver them?"

"At our earliest convenience," replied Puffy, who couldn't help noticing the smile on his captain's face.

"What grade of Blacks are we to take?" asked Captain Cumulus.

"Four-star," was the reply.

That was a tall order. For most purposes sea water, or brine as it was sometimes known, only had a one-star rating but would do. They would have to consult the *Water Rating Manual* to locate the nearest source of four-star water.

"The nearest source is Lake Ullswater, so we will set off first thing after nightfall."

Making Preparation

Later that evening, Captain Cumulus steered the *Nimbus* through a moonless night sky in a northerly direction towards the Lake District. He steered not by compass but with a device called a soakometer. The first four letters of the word stood for "Search, Overland, Absorb, and Karry". The device was an early form of a navigation aid. The latitude and longitude of both the starting point and destination had to be punched in on its keyboard, and it would get the cloud machine to where the captain wanted to be. The Absorb function had been disabled and had to be carried out separately upon arrival these days. On a murky night like this one, it was good to have a navigation aid, or nav-aid, to do the work.

Down below, a huge cloud convoy made up of Cumberland Greys and Westmorland Whites masked the ground. They looked very solid from the *Nimbus. They are probably heading for the Midlands and should reach there by morning,* mused the captain.

Puffy concentrated on observing the instruments, which gave an indication of how the fan duct motors that propelled the Nimbus were performing. As he was doing so, Captain Cumulus lifted a jug from a shelf and poured himself a drink.

There he goes again, thought Puffy, who had spotted the captain in the corner of his eye. *Every time he gets a job over Holland, he takes a drink from the jug marked "Rob's tea". He's a weird man!*

"Okay, Puffy, switch her to hover," shouted the captain. They had arrived over Ullswater just after midnight, and as luck would have it, a gap had occurred in the Cumberland Greys and Westmorland Whites to reveal the inky black lake below. "Switch on the atomiser and set it to absorb four million gallons."

"Aye, aye, Captain."

It would take the *Nimbus* an hour to convert four million gallons of Ullswater into cloud. It was then up to the captain, hidden with his engineer Puffy in the bullet-shaped Cloud Machine in the very centre of the cloud, to decide what size, shape, and colour it would be for the journey to Holland.

The hour passed slowly—much to the annoyance of the captain, who was anxious to get going and showed it by pacing on the foredeck.

Puffy couldn't help thinking, *Here we go again. Every time we go to Holland, he gets all anxious and irritable. I wonder what it all means.*

A Hiccup on the Journey

Eventually the *Nimbus* was loaded, and she ascended to three thousand feet to begin the journey east toward Holland.

"What shape do you want us to be, Captain?" asked Puffy.

"Set us for large and thunderous," came the reply.

"That means we need to be black as well!"

"That's it, Puffy, black as well."

For the first few hours all went well. They sailed in the night sky, mingling with the Cumberland Greys and Westmorland Whites on their way to the Midlands. Suddenly the whole sky was lit up by a bolt of lightning which, for an instant, linked a couple of clouds. Seconds later there was the expected clap of thunder, which severely rocked both the control unit of the *Nimbus* and the nerves of her crew.

"Shiver me trouser belt and twang me braces," cried Puffy. "That was loud and ferocious."

The captain never blinked an eyelid. He had sailed through electric storms before, and anyway, they would be setting a course for Scheveningen on the Dutch coast any moment now. Consequently they would leave their present companions to make their way to the Midlands.

"Captain!" shouted Puffy.

"What is it, Puffy?"

"We have ascended another 1,500 feet, but I haven't made any adjustments to the motors."

"That's strange," replied the captain, who then proceeded to scan the instruments in order to ascertain a reason for the present state of affairs. "Well, well! We have lost 250 gallons of water," he remarked.

"I wonder where it went?"

In the next few moments, the phone rang.

"Hello! This is the *Nimbus* speaking."

"Are you the great big black job immediately above us?" said the voice through the earpiece.

"That depends," replied the captain. "Who are you, and where are you calling from?"

"This is Horace from the Hull Weather Centre, and I want to know what you are doing over here, giving us a drenching. You're not forecast! There's nothing on my charts to indicate that you are passing this way. We haven't even announced you. People were not prepared for you. It just isn't on!"

Captain Cumulus cautiously peered through his periscope to ascertain precisely where they were. Sure enough, immediately below them was the city of Hull, on the northern banks of the River Humber. The captain replied, "Sorry, Horace, the *Nimbus* is directly above you, but we shouldn't have given you a drenching. We seem to have developed a problem. We sailed through a thunderstorm a little earlier, and it may have caused some damage."

"Where is the *Nimbus* headed, Captain?"

"She's bound for Holland with Manchester Blacks."

"The poor blighters," remarked Horace. "Anyway, clear off my patch and go and drench the Dutch."

A Crisis Averted

"If we are going to maintain this altitude, Captain, we'd better reduce our motor power," commented Puffy.

The captain agreed and started to adjust the throttle. "It's stuck—I can't budge the thing!" he exclaimed.

For the next few hours, the captain struggled in vain to move the throttle control, and the *Nimbus* climbed ever higher as she lightened her load by drenching the North Sea as she passed over.

"There's the coast of Holland," cried Puffy.

"We are at an altitude of six thousand feet now, Puffy. At this rate, by the time we get to Apeldoorn we will be too high up for rain. We'll only be able to produce slush, and that's not what we have been contracted for."

"What are we going to do, Captain?" asked Puffy.

"There's only one thing for it: we'll have to call in Polak's Cloud Engineers in Arnhem and see what they can do for us."

"Hallo, dit is Polak's Werks. Ik ben Mienke, meneer Polak's secretarresse. Wat kan ik voor u doen?"

"This is Captain Cumulus speaking aboard the Cloud Machine *Nimbus*. I'm taking a load of Manchester Blacks to Apeldoorn, but I have a problem. The *Nimbus* has sprung a leak, and the throttle has stuck. We are steadily climbing, and by the time we reach Apeldoorn, we will only be able to give them slush."

"I shall put you through to our technical director, Jan Zoutendijk," replied Mienke in near perfect English.

The captain and Jan Zoutendijk discussed the problem at length. Finally, the captain put down the phone and turned to Puffy. "Within the hour we shall rendezvous over Utrecht with one of Polak's ballast clouds, so keep your eyes open."

Clever people, these Dutch, thought Puffy. *They can control water on land and in the sky. Trouble is that theirs is probably too salty; that's why they have to import our stuff.*

Upon approaching Utrecht, they could see a distinctly portly looking cloud coming towards them. It was slightly higher than the *Nimbus* and was obviously fairly heavy because it had an inky black colour.

The phone rang, and Captain Cumulus answered it.

"Dit is Captain Hans spreking. I am aboard Polak's ballast cloud, de *Ellinchem*. In five minutes we will be above you, and then we will descend on top of you and steadily push you down to three thousand feet as you approach Apeldoorn. Be prepared for a bump."

Captain Cumulus and Puffy braced themselves. When the bump came, it was relatively minor compared with what they had experienced in the thunderstorm. They descended slowly on the journey to Apeldoorn, but the captain could be well pleased! He would now be able to deliver his Manchester Blacks. The *Nimbus* still had 4,950,000 gallons of its original load of four-star Ullswater.

With Apeldoorn just ahead, Puffy inquired whether it was time to set the rain control, and if so, on what setting. The captain mused over the decision. He could give the populace of the town intermittent light rain, steady drizzle, heavy rain, or a torrential downpour. However, he had a special soft spot for the place and couldn't resist being as gentle as he could whilst at the same time producing rain that would be consistent with the image of the *Nimbus.* "Set her for light rain, Puffy."

"Aye aye, Captain."

The rain fell on Apeldoorn, and the captain watched with what appeared to be a mixture of pleasure and sadness. Even when the *Nimbus* had fully unloaded, the captain continued to stare out from the foredeck.

"Shall we set sail for home now, Captain?" asked Puffy.

They bade farewell to Polak's ballast cloud *Ellinchem* after having thanked its Captain, and they watched it lift off the *Nimbus* and head back to Arnhem. The captain set a course for England, and for the first time in history he invited Puffy to a drink of Rob's tea.

By Jove, that's mighty fine tea! thought Puffy

The two cloud mariners drifted off into their private worlds and forgot all about the *Nimbus,* which by now was very light indeed and had ascended to a heavenly altitude, for the throttle was still stuck.

At this rate the *Nimbus* should be in orbit just after midnight, but who cared? Puffy and the captain were celebrating a job well done—and at Apeldoorn, too!

THE GREAT CLOUD PARADE

By Royal Command

Captain Cumulus was sitting in his front room, twiddling his thumbs and wondering how he could fill his time. This Monday had all the hallmarks of the start of another boring week. It was a time in his life when not much was happening, and one week was no different from any other—in fact life was becoming tedious. He had done little work with his Cloud Machine, the *Nimbus*, for some time, and it was currently lying dormant, anchored in a large hangar at Wythenshawe Weather Centre.

Puffy White, the engineer serving on the *Nimbus* and the lifetime friend of Captain Cumulus, popped into the room with a copy of a newspaper in his hand. "Here you are, Captain. Something for you to read and help pass the time."

"A copy of the *Daily Gloom*, eh? Something to top up my depression, no doubt," answered Captain Cumulus.

Puffy handed over the paper and, sensing the Captain's mood, made a quick departure, thinking that a cup of tea and a bacon butty in the kitchen would be a better option than keeping the captain company.

Looking through the paper revealed the usual items that generally reinforced the Captain's jaundiced view of life in England today: the economic crisis, the need to cut back on government spending and what that meant for Joe Public, and the need to pay bankers millions of pounds in bonuses. Murders, robberies, and anti-social behaviour—in other words, all those things that depress people with time to dwell on them—were featured on a substantial number of pages.

While scanning through the adverts, sports, and various other things that adorned the pages, the captain's eyes were drawn to a notice on page eleven.

By Royal Command

> All grade 1, 2, and 3 Cloud Machine owners are to report to the Wythenshawe Weather Centre on Wednesday, March 14, 2012 at 10.00 am prompt.
>
> Owners who fail to attend without appropriate dispensation will forfeit their licences to manufacture clouds and may be subject to payment of fines.
>
> Each owner is to report on arrival to the superintendant in charge, Mr I. N. Spite, CDM.

The Captain was about to shout for Puffy when the phone rang. "Hello, Captain Cumulus speaking."

The voice said, "Don't give me all that Captain nonsense, Cirrus!" Cirrus Cumulus was the captain's full name. "What do you make of that Royal Command in today's paper?"

"Is that Windy Blower?" asked the captain.

"You know it is, Cirrus, so stop mucking about and answer the question," replied Windy.

"Frankly, I have no idea what the Command is all about. Have you tried contacting anyone else?"

Windy had tried contacting several other Cloud Machine owners, but nobody could shed any light on why everybody was being summoned to attend the Weather Centre in this very formal way. There were, as usual, many rumours—Cloud Machines were going to have MOT tests, new pilot exams were being introduced, the government was going to introduce a new VART tax (value added rain tax), there were new laws being introduced limiting what Cloud Machines were allowed to do, and more—but the real truth was that no one really knew what was going on.

Wythenshawe Weather Centre

Puffy and the captain arrived at Wythenshawe Weather Centre early on the appointed Wednesday morning so that they could check on the security of the *Nimbus*, their much-valued Cloud Machine. The hangar in which it was housed was vast and could easily have accommodated the great airships of the 1920s. Inside was awe-inspiring. The great height of the ceiling and the many visible girders upon which the outer skin of the building were attached gave a feeling of security, and the echoes generated when people spoke added to the impression of enormity.

Along each side of the hangar were anchored a row of naked Cloud Machines, something that the general public could not see because in their natural environment they would be the nucleus of whatever type of cloud they were making at the time. In the naked form each machine looked something like a bullet, but a bit more bulbous in the middle. Around the outside were mounted four fan duct motors, each looking like a propeller with many blades inside a swivelling metal tube. There were two of these on each side of the hull, and they could produce thrust of varying strength and direction.

A television camera was mounted in a kind of periscope on top of the craft to provide the captain with forward vision and it could also be rotated to give all around vision. The hull also had a number of lumps that housed a variety of equipment. There was one for parachutes on the top, in case of a catastrophe. There was one to house the radio antennae and one for the identification beacon. The beacon was a device which allowed each Cloud Machine to be identified on the screen of a PPI in the pilot's cockpit.

Although each Cloud Machine looked similar, some were much bigger than others, and they were not all the same colour. The older machines no longer had distinctive paintwork and had stains around the many grill-covered holes out of which the cloud vapour was discharged when work was being done. The one thing they all had in common was that they had been manufactured by Black, Black & Blakemore's in their factory in deeper Salford.

After having looked over the *Nimbus* and satisfied themselves that all was well, Puffy and Captain Cumulus made their way into the Weather Centre office block. They entered the building and followed the signs that led them to a conference hall. At the entrance was a table with a large sheet of paper upon it. Sitting at the table was an official who insisted they sign the paper in the appropriate place and provide evidence of Cloud Machine ownership.

The two crew members signed their names in the spaces associated with the *Nimbus* and entered the cavernous conference hall, which had a stage at one end and tiers of cinema-type seats, set back a little from the stage edge and then rising toward the opposite end wall. On the stage sat a number of official-looking people, including the superintendent, Mr I. N. Spite, CDM. Each official had a microphone and papers placed on a table in front of him or her.

In the hall had gathered between thirty and forty Cloud Machine owners by the time Puffy and Captain Cumulus arrived. The *Nimbus* crew recognized several of them: Sunny Blue, skipper of the *Flier*; Snowy White, skipper of the *Dismal;* and of course Windy Blower, whose machine was named *Spitting*. Much to the embarrassment of Captain Cumulus, Windy would insist on calling him Cirrus, which roused considerable amusement amongst those assembled.

There was a great deal of speculation as to what was about to transpire, and when Mr I. N. Spite rose from his seat, a sudden hush descended on those assembled.

"Cloud Machine owners, ladies and gentleman," began Mr Spite. "Her Majesty the Queen has instructed me to gather you all here today."

At this point there was a combination of whispers and movement as individuals attempted conversations, but this rapidly ceased as Mr Spite continued. "On June 2, 2012, there will be a Great Cloud Parade that will take place at Hoghton Tower in Lancashire, just southeast of Preston. The parade will take the form of a flypast, with the queen taking the salute."

An excited buzz reverberated around the hall. This was something never done before, and it was certainly something to brighten the day for Captain Cirrus Cumulus.

"First, let me deal with the formation of the flypast. There will be three waves of clouds. The first wave will be made up of nine grade-one machines flying in the form of an arrowhead. Each machine will travel in the form of a Westmorland White cloud. The leader at the head of the arrow will be Captain Cumulus in the *Nimbus.* On each side of the *Nimbus,* trailing back and spaced five hundred feet apart, will be four other grade-one machines, the details of which you can obtain on your way out."

Both Captain Cumulus and Puffy where delighted with the honour of leading the formation flypast. The production of Westmorland White clouds, the puffy white jobs that are used to decorate blue skies, was well within the capabilities of the *Nimbus.*

Mr Spite continued. "The second wave will consist of three columns of grade-two machines flying in the form of Cumberland Greys. Each column will be made up of five machines separated by five hundred feet. One column will follow the trailing edge of each end of the arrow formation, whilst the third will be in between the two outer columns. The leader of the second wave will be at the head of the centre column and will be Abigail Windrush in the *Hurricane.*

"The third and final wave will consist of fifteen grade-three machines in the form of Manchester Blacks. There will be three lateral parallel rows of five, and each cloud will extend vertically before taking the classical shape of an anvil. The leader in the centre position of the first row will be Windy Blower in the *Spitting.*

"Natural weather conditions on the day will have to meet certain conditions. Any natural cloud must be no lower than fifteen thousand feet and wind speed no greater than thirty knots, which would exceed the operating limits of your machines. For special effects, in wave two the last two in the outer columns can give off a little drizzle. In wave three the outer machines in row two can provide thunder and lightning, with the lightning being in red, white, and blue. In row three the two outer machines are to supply heavy rain and good angel rays." This was going to be something of a challenge, and no doubt several rehearsals would be required. "Ladies and gentleman, you will have one week in which to prepare your machines, and then you will depart for Jurby in the Isle of Man, where you can practise as separate waves and gradually build up to the full formation of three. When you are proficient in formation flying, you will practise flypasts at Silloth in Cumbria. You must be ready by May 25."

Mr Spite ended by asking for any questions, but a very excited Captain Cumulus couldn't wait to get back home and start planning for the task in hand.

Rehearsing in the Isle-of-Man

By March 22, some thirty-nine Cloud Machines had gathered at the disused airfield at Jurby in the Isle of Man, which fortunately had enough old hangars to accommodate them all. When not in use, the machines would be kept in the hangars to maintain secrecy as much as possible before the big day. Each wave was allocated a building in which the wave leader could gather together the full complement of pilots and plan how the job was to be accomplished.

Each day before dawn, the Cloud Machines would get airborne and proceed in a westerly direction over the Irish Sea. They would then switch on their atomisers to take on board the quantity of sea water required, in vaporised form, to convert into ice for storage onboard until required for cloud making. Once loaded up, each machine would head back in an easterly direction before using their sublimators to change the ice into cloud vapour, which would then discharge through the many grill-covered portholes around the bullet-shaped hull to envelop it in the cloud form allocated. In the case of the *Nimbus*, this was a beautiful, swan-like Westmorland White.

It was at this juncture that the TV cameras came into their own, and a screen in the cockpit provided the view of outside for the pilot. A second screen took the form of a PPI, (or plan position indicator), which provided a very useful image showing where all the other clouds were, hence allowing pilots to avoid collisions. This latter equipment received its information from the identification beacon onboard each Cloud Machine, and it was regarded as most valuable. There was nothing worse to see than a dented cloud or one with mixed shades of white, grey, and black. People like to know where they are with clouds. In the most calamitous cases, a collision may result in the Cloud Machines themselves impacting, resulting in a rapid descent to earth surrounded by the foulest of weather. Fortunately this was a very rare occurrence.

When in cloud form, each wave would proceed to an allocated area to practise its own formation. The first wave would return to overhead Jurby. The second would proceed to the disused airfield at Andreas, which was northeast of Jurby. The third, which was in the form of the more menacing Manchester Blacks, was allocated a position offshore, just north of the Point-of-Ayr. This location had been arranged in order not to induce any great anxiety amongst the local population. Any impending storms would be seen as missing the island, at least with a bit of luck.

Rehearsals had to be confined to those days when the natural clouds were above fifteen thousand feet and the wind speed did not exceed thirty knots. On many days that was not the case, and it was May 10 before the individual wave formations could be judged proficient. On those days when flying was not possible, the crews did some considerable socialising, some of which was best not referred to. Suffice it to say that beer supplies on the island were in short supply until sometime after the crews had departed for Silloth.

Captain Cumulus in the *Nimbus* and his eight colleagues assembled overhead Jurby airfield to perform rehearsals. It was a relatively easy start because the first objective was to get everybody in the right position, and this was achieved by being stationary over a ground observer, who communicated positioning data using a radio transmitter. Each Cloud Machine tuned in to a common frequency, 175.3, to receive instructions, and each had been given a number. The *Nimbus* was naturally number one, those to his right were two to five, and those to his left were six to nine.

"Number three, move forward a bit; number seven, back a bit; number four, to the left a bit." These were the instructions from the ground to get the positions just right. The *Nimbus* had a vertical separation indicator (VSI), which allowed the wave leader, Captain Cumulus, to get everyone on the same level. All this positioning was not totally free from problems because the wind would often try to upset matters, and each pilot had to carefully juggle the fan duct motors to counteract the effect.

"Cirrus, the formation looks good," said Puffy, taking a look at the TV screen and PPI on the cockpit control console over the skipper's shoulder.

"It's Captain to you," pointed out Cirrus in a gruff voice. "But it does look good, I'll grant you that," he added in a more conciliatory tone. "It's time, I think, to start the formation in motion."

The next rehearsals saw the first wave maintaining formation whilst performing a slow circuit of the old airfield. Everyone maintaining the same height was not a problem, but keeping station needed some practice. For a left-hand turn, number nine had to slow down having the smallest turning arc, whilst number five had the greatest arc and needed to accelerate considerably. The opposite was required for a right-hand turn. At first there were some ragged formations after turning, as well as one or two minor collisions which resulted in a few dented Westmorland Whites, but it was nothing too serious. The key to it all was careful but skilful operation of the four fan duct motors. Like everything else, practise makes perfect.

It was a similar story over at Andreas, where wave two leader, Abigail Windrush in the *Hurricane,* was rehearsing with her fourteen colleagues. She had started in the same fashion with a stationary formation, using a ground observer. The difference here was that each machine was enveloped in a Cumberland Grey, which were somewhat larger than the decorative Westmorland Whites. Added to this was the fact that each of the three long, parallel columns was made up of five clouds, and more ground space was covered, rendering observation by a single ground observer impractical. They overcame this issue by using three observers, one at the head of the columns, one at the rear, and one in the middle. Abigail had tried using a helicopter flying above the clouds, but the down draught from its rotor blades proved too much to handle and resulted in one cloud being forced to descend to ground level speedily—and it coincided with village girl Molly Ramsey, just departing the local fish and chip shop, walking into a lamp standard. The sudden arrival of dense cloud was like the sudden arrival of a sea mist, and Molly had been lost in the midst of it and hadn't seen the obstacle. When the cloud suddenly lifted, Molly could see that her dad's pie and chips were adorning the pavement whilst a flock of seagulls happily looked on. Her dad was not impressed with her story!

Abigail was eventually able to move her cloud wave onto slow circuit flying, and she had the same difficulties initially as Captain Cumulus, but with practise she was happy with the good formation achieved. In time, both waves one and two could perform circuits at ground speeds of twenty knots in a variety of natural wind states.

Wave two performed a limited number of rehearsals with special effects, which involved the last clouds in the two outer rows turning on drizzle for set periods of time. The problem with this was that as the wave formation passed over the same ground positions on each circuit, the same people received the rain each time. It was not long before a number of irate locals, suffering from wet washing on the line and a disgruntled wedding party in the middle of a photo shoot, made vociferous complaints. The special effects were temporarily suspended.

On the subject of special effects, the *Nimbus* crew's engineer, Puffy White, had the super idea of suspending below the *Nimbus* a Union Jack flag on a weighted line, and this was duly done. The skipper couldn't see the flag on his screen and had to rely on the ground controller, but the task was mastered.

The populace of Jurby and Andreas were not unduly inquisitive about the orbiting cloud formations, apart from the drizzle. When all is said and done, if you see cats with three legs, there's nothing so strange about orbiting clouds—although one with a flag under it is a bit strange!

Wave three, led by Windy Blower in the *Spitting*, was a far more menacing spectacle, and there was good logic involved in allocating an area out at sea for rehearsals. The large, voluminous, anvil-shaped Manchester Blacks always had the menacing look of a storm about to break. Windy's rehearsal system was the same as the others: stationary formation-keeping first and then slow circuits, steadily building up to twenty knots. There was of course the problem of ground observers, but they overcame it by using the Point-of-Ayr lighthouse keeper and Ramsey lifeboat, which most obligingly positioned itself strategically using a GPS set.

Special effects worked admirably well. The outer clouds in the rear lateral row had no problem creating a downpour, and with the light in the right position, the sticks of rain connecting cloud and earth, known in younger circles as angel rays, were clearly visible. Coloured thunder and lightning was altogether another thing. To produce the lightning, Van de Graaf generators had been installed in the machines that would form the middle row in the outer positions. These generators, when wound up, would develop a bigger and bigger electrical charge until it was of such magnitude that it forced a strike of current between itself and mother earth—in other words, a bolt of lightning. A thunderous recording would be broadcast through onboard loudspeakers a few seconds after the lightning strike. This would be repeated three times, and the lightning would be in the form of three strikes in red, white, and then blue. It was the colouring of the strikes which had given the engineers at Black, Black & Blackemore's in deeper Salford the biggest headache. In the end it had been solved by attaching three dye-filled tanks connected to what looked like a water pistol attached to each of the Van de Graaf generators. Each tank was triggered in turn to supply the pistol that would inject its contents into the lightning flash, and hey presto—coloured lightning, and to great effect!

The thunder and coloured lightning brought large numbers of people from the village of Bride to witness the rehearsals, and several inquiries were made regarding what the phenomenon was, but no answers were forthcoming because this was a secret operation.

By May 10 Captain Cumulus, Abigail Windrush, and Windy Blower were satisfied that their objectives had been achieved. It was now time to bring them all together. The move to Silloth was about to take place.

The Final Stage of Training at Silloth

On Thursday night, May 11, all thirty-nine of the Cloud Machines made their way individually across the Irish Sea to Cumbria under the cover of darkness. Those attached to the first two waves, a total of twenty-four, landed at the disused coastal airfield at Silloth; the remaining fifteen carried on a little further inland to another disused airfield at Kirkbride. Each location had ample hangar space to accommodate all the machines, and because they were situated next to the Solway Firth, there was an ample supply of water, the essential ingredient for cloud making. It was important to crack on with rehearsals because only three weeks remained to the royal flypast, and everyone would have to pray for suitable weather conditions.

Captain Cumulus decided that he would rehearse over Silloth with waves one and two to begin with. He'd leave wave three to its own devices at Kirkbride until he had perfected the bigger formation.

It didn't take long for waves one and two to join up and maintain good station, at least whilst they were stationary; the use of ground observers helped considerably. Maintaining station whilst in motion initially hit a snag. Whilst performing a circuit that took the formation out over the Solway Firth, the formation turned into a strong headwind, and before everyone had adjusted their fan duct motors, the clouds started to bunch up. There was a collision between the two middle machines in the centre column of wave two. The latter machine suffered damage to its TV camera, rendering its skipper, Al Blighty, blind and soaked by the contents of a cup of tea he had placed on top of his instrument panel. Al went into a rage and, using words for which no spelling had been invented, cursed the skipper in front. Then with guidance from a ground controller, he headed back to Silloth for repairs. Within twenty-four hours, engineers from Black, Black & Blackemore's in deeper Salford arrived and fitted a new camera. After this hiccup, rehearsals went well, and all the skippers rapidly became adept at keeping station with skilful adjustment of the fan duct motors.

By May 18, Captain Cumulus was satisfied that wave three could join the others in rehearsal. Provided the weather held, he would have everything ready for the big day. Because of the increased length of the formation created by having all three waves behind each other, the captain decided that they would form up over the Solway Firth. To get the stationary formation correct, he decided to hire a few boats from Maryport, just down the coast, and put the ground controllers in them. As before, it didn't take long to get the stationary formation up to scratch, and soon they practised circuits.

Captain Cumulus got all the skippers together one evening in the old briefing room at Silloth to outline his final training routine. "Now this is the plan," he began. "We will form up over the Solway Firth and proceed in an easterly direction until we have almost reached the Navy Radio Station at Anthorn, at which point we will make a ninety-degree turn to starboard to enter the area on your charts marked Moricambe. We will proceed down the Moricambe for a short distance before making another ninety-degree turn to starboard to bring us down the main runway at Silloth Airfield, where observers have been placed on the old control tower to simulate the queen taking the salute. After flying over the airfield, we will continue on the same heading until we have passed Silloth town on our starboard side, before making another ninety-degree starboard turn to get us back over the Solway Firth. Now, are there any questions?"

There was a hum about the room. Clearly the whole exercise was getting near to its execution.

"What height are we going to fly at, Cirrus?" asked Windy Blower.

The captain, clearly aggravated by being called by his first name, held his dignity and replied, "We will start at 500 feet, and as we perfect things we will descend to the display height of 250 feet."

"What will be our ground speed, Captain?" asked Abigail Windrush.

In a much more relaxed manner, the captain replied, "Twenty-five knots Abigail. If we make it any slower, it will make the flypast too slow, and we don't want the queen getting cold."

"What about the special effects?" chirped in Puffy White.

"As soon as we can operate at 250 feet, we will test the special effects."

With all questions answered, everyone retired to get an early night before the final rehearsals started.

Given all the careful preparation that had already gone into the flypast, it was not long before the thirty-nine clouds were making a spectacular display over Silloth airfield. The observer situated on the old control tower representing the queen had a first-class view of everything. Coming down the old main runway from a north-easterly direction at 250 feet were the nine Westmorland White clouds in an arrowhead formation, moving gracefully at twenty-five knots with the *Nimbus* right on the runway centre line—a brilliant bit of precision flying. Following on from wave one came wave two in three columns of five Cumberland Greys, portraying a possible weather change. The first waves of clouds did not extend outside the boundaries of the old airfield. The same could not be said of wave three, made up of fifteen Manchester Blacks in three lines abreast. These clouds, much bigger than the others, extended out a considerable distance on either side of the airfield boundary, so much so that the three end clouds on the right-hand side of the formation flew right over the top of Silloth town as the whole formation proceeded on its south-westerly heading to cross the airfield.

The group made the decision to invite the local community to witness a final rehearsal of the Great Cloud Parade on May 31, including special effects. The local mayor and his good lady viewed the proceedings from the control tower veranda, and everyone else gathered on either side of the main runway. There was a great expectancy, and excited schoolchildren constantly scanned the skies to pick out the cloud flypast formation from all the other clouds powdering the face of the blue sky, and they were not in short supply that day. As the time for the cloud parade approached, viewers spotted the formation north-west of the airfield over the Solway Firth, heading inland. What had made it possible to pick it out was the low height at which it was approaching and the different direction it was travelling in comparison with the natural clouds.

At 11.00 am on the dot, the *Nimbus* led the parade across the airfield, complete with a Union Jack flag under its Westmorland White configuration. As the first wave passed overhead, the second followed in the form of Cumberland Greys with an accompanying reduction in light. The last cloud in each outer row drizzled on the airfield, but no one complained. Then came the more menacing Manchester Blacks, and the sky became a lot darker. The clouds stretched out to the left and right as far as anyone could see. The second line abreast was spectacular, being accompanied by thunder and then frightening bolts of coloured lightning; fortunately the lightning was outside the airfield boundary. The final line abreast of Manchester Blacks came next, with the outer ones pouring rain. The natural light illuminated the rain sticks to create pretty-looking angel rays that had the children in complete awe. The crowd's heads followed the moving clouds and watched them head off to the south-west and then out over the Solway Firth.

The end of the Great Cloud Parade was greeted by an enormous outburst of enthusiasm and praise, and there was no doubt that this was a memorable event that would be passed on from generation to generation in the small town of Silloth.

Not everything had gone smoothly, however. The lightning had played havoc with the operation of the Navy Radio Station at Anthorn, and the Admiralty made a strong protest. The downpour had given a number of holidaymakers on Silloth promenade a thorough soaking, and there were a number of irate people in town that night who were not happy with the fact that they had not been told what to expect. In spite of all this, Captain Cumulus was able to inform Mr I.N.Spite at Wythenshawe Weather Centre that he was ready for the big day.

The Big Day Arrives

June 2 turned out to be a beautiful day with a clear blue sky and only a slight southerly wind; it was as if everybody's prayers had been answered. At Hoghton Tower preparations for this day had been going on for weeks. No such event as the one about to take place on this special day had been seen here since King James I, at a banquet held in his honour, famously knighted a loin of beef 'Sir Loin'.

The long drive to the Tower from the main road dipped down before rising steadily to the top of a hill, upon which the imposing tower stands. On each side of the drive, set back a little, rows of trees extended almost the whole distance before giving way to an acre or two of a well-cut grassed area that stretched to the outer walls. Entrance to the Tower was by an arched, double wooden gate set back in a two-storey stone tower, upon which stood a second slightly smaller tower with flags on top. The queen and her escorts would view the Great Cloud Parade from a prominent position on the lower tower.

Grenadier Guards in red tunics lined the long drive, and the many flags that had been erected fluttered in the light breeze. Behind the Guards, a great many people had gathered to witness the spectacle that was about to take place; ice cream and food vendors did a roaring trade.

The world-famous Leyland Brass Band had assembled to the right of the Tower entrance. They were regaled in their white tunics and entertained the crowd that had gathered.

At 1.30 pm precisely, the queen's limousine turned into the long driveway. The Guards gave the royal salute, and the crowds cheered as she was graciously transported to Hoghton Tower. Leyland Band played the national anthem as Her Majesty stepped out of the royal limousine and into the warm but fresh Lancashire air. After being introduced to a number of local dignitaries, the Guards escorted her to the stone stairway inside the entrance tunnel in order to ascend to the roof position, from where she would take the salute from the *Nimbus* leading a monumental flypast of Westmorland Whites, Cumberland Greys, and Manchester Blacks. The scene was set!

The night before, at Silloth, Captain Cumulus and his faithful engineer, Puffy, clambered on board the *Nimbus*. At the same time the other Cloud Machines were mounted by their respective crews; the same was also happening at Kirkbride. The object was to get all the machines airborne whilst it was still dark and then fly down the Cumbria coast and across the entrance of Morecambe Bay to a position in the Irish Sea west of Blackpool. If they could reach this location early enough, they could activate their respective atomisers to take on board sea water and then vaporise it to create the cloud that had been ascribed to them.

The fan duct motors on each Cloud Machine were silent running, except when being adjusted to determine the direction they were to go in, which resulted in a blowing wind sound. When some twenty-four machines got airborne simultaneously and manoeuvred, the sound was something akin to a whirlwind, but fortunately the good folk of Silloth—and for that matter, Kirkbride—were not awakened. The whole entourage of bullet-shaped machines, totalling thirty-nine, made good their short journey to the west and over the Solway Firth.

Once over the Solway, the machines headed south with the Cumbria coast on their port side. The twinkling lights on the mainland looked rather pretty, and the crews could make out towns as clusters of light that tended to create a halo above them. Maryport, Workington, and Whitehaven could easily be picked out, and then came Ravenglass and finally Barrow-in-Furness, which was the brightest of all. A black abyss followed as the machines flew across the mouth of Morecambe Bay, although it was true to say that in the distance the lights of Lancaster could just be made out, and there were lights ahead marking the position of Fleetwood, which generated a strong smell of fish in everyone's nostrils.

The flight along the coast from Fleetwood to Blackpool was a relatively short affair, and picking a point opposite Blackpool's famous tower to come to a halt was not difficult because its illumination made it impossible to miss. By good fortune and good luck, the thirty-nine machines arrived at the agreed position and began the process of atomisation well before dawn broke. Fledgling clouds began to envelop each Cloud Machine as the dawn chorus began, and first light revealed to anyone that cared to look out to sea a strange gaggle of assorted clouds, for they had not got into formation for the flypast at this point.

Now was an opportunity to take a breather whilst Captain Cumulus formulated his flight plan to take the formation over Hoghton Tower at exactly 2.00 pm, which was 1400 hours in flight planners' talk! Once this was done, everyone would move to the start position and form up with the aid of ground observers once more. This bit was all pre-planned, and the RNLI lifeboats from Lytham St Anne's, Blackpool, and Fleetwood would rendezvous with them when called to do so.

The captain was a fastidious planner and was determined to make everything go exactly right. He placed the relevant chart on his navigator's table and mused for a while. He noted the location of Hoghton Tower—latitude 53°44' north, longitude 2°36' west. He then drew a straight line westwards from Hoghton Tower that extended out over the Irish Sea, and as it did so, it passed over two useful way marks: first was Junction 30, where the M6 and the M61 motorways merged, and second was the point at which the River Douglas ran into the River Ribble. These would be easily observable and were a good check that he was keeping on track. The line then continued down the centre of the River Ribble and out into the Irish Sea. The captain determined that the start point for the run-in to Hoghton Tower would be at latitude 53°44' north, longitude 3°10' west, which would make it 34 nautical miles in distance. If the formation flew at an indicated airspeed of twenty knots, that would be one nautical mile every three minutes it would take one hour forty-two minutes to reach their destination. For a 1400 hours arrival, they would have to start off at 1218 hours.

The choice of start would be a good one because it would be far enough away from the coast not to give anything away, and the special effects could be checked out with a degree of security. But there were some more details to work out, the heading to fly on using the compass on board the *Nimbus,* for a start. The captain worked this out using his navigator's protractor and determined from his chart that the heading would be 102° magnetic which meant it was heading east-south-east. Next was the height at which to fly. To allow everybody at Hoghton Tower to get a good view of the flypast, and to be able to see each separate cloud without them appearing to merge, it was decided that a minimum height of 500 feet would be ideal, in spite of the display height being originally 250 feet. However, because the tower was 800 feet above sea level, Captain Cumulus would need to lead his formation at 1,300 feet to give the appropriate clearance.

That is just about it for now, thought the Captain. The Cloud Machines could move to the start position in about one hour using the global positioning satellite system and form up. Once that was done, contact with the weather people should provide the latest information on wind speed and direction and the atmospheric pressure, which was important for setting the altimeter. Warton aerodrome was on the port side of the flight track on the northern bank of the River Ribble, and because the formation would pass through Warton's control zone, it would be important to liaise with them. There was certainly a lot to this flight-planning business.

"How's the plan coming along, Captain?" asked Puffy.

"Just about finished," replied the captain. "We can have a cup of tea and then move off to the start position."

Some things never change, thought Puffy.

Shortly, Captain Cumulus called up all the other Cloud Machines on his radio using the agreed frequency, 175.3. "This is Captain Cumulus speaking. All machines are to progress immediately to latitude 53°44' north, longitude 3°10' west and form up into your formation positions. Acknowledge."

One by one, each of the other thirty-eight machines acknowledged and then began to move off to the prescribed location.

"Puffy, contact the RNLI and give them the co-ordinates. Tell them I need them to be in position by 1100 hours, and once they observe our form-up, they are to place themselves under the front, rear, and middle waves."

"Aye aye, Captain," said Puffy, feeling the first tinge of excitement as the big moment approached.

The captain eyed his watch because timing was so important.

In due course all the Cloud Machines arrived at the position given to them by the formation leader. The use of their GPS equipment made the exercise relatively easy. On arrival, each machine turned to face the mainland and moved into their approximate positions. Nine class-one machines in the form of Westmorland Whites were in arrowhead formation with the *Nimbus* at the very head. Fifteen class-two machines in the form of Cumberland Greys were in three parallel columns of five, with Abigail Windrush in the *Hurricane* at the head of the middle column. Finally, fifteen class-three machines were in the form of Manchester Blacks and moved in three parallel lateral rows of five, with Windy Blower in the *Spitting* in the middle of the front row.

"All machines are to report in using the agreed procedure." Captain Cumulus issued the instruction over the radio, and one by one, each responded.

"Wave one, number two, present and correct."

"Wave one, number three, present and correct."

"Wave two, number five, present and correct."

"Wave three, number six, present and correct."

And so on, until, "Wave three, number fifteen, present and correct."

Satisfied that everyone was present, the captain thought it was time to make use of the ground observers. Lytham St Anne's lifeboat had positioned itself under wave one and proceeded to issue a stream of instructions. "Number three, move forward a bit, hold it. Number five, back a bit, hold it. Number seven, move to the left a bit, hold it," As this went on, the Blackpool lifeboat was doing the same with wave two, and the lifeboat from Fleetwood assisted wave three.

The formation was almost ready, and it was at this point that Captain Cumulus, using his radio, asked for weather information. Back came the details he needed: a southerly wind at four knots, and an atmospheric pressure of 1019 millibars. The last bit of information was called a QNH, and it was the air pressure at sea level. The air pressure was duly fed into the altimeter on the cockpit console, and the Captain now knew accurately his height above the sea. The QNH was relayed by the *Nimbus* to all the other machines, and as they fed the information into their respective altimeters, it became obvious that they were not all at the same height—and no one was at 1,300 feet. The captain gave the instruction for the whole formation to ascend to the flypast height, and they complied, although it must be said that a fair amount of bobbing up and down occurred before all the machines shared the same horizontal plane; over the air waves a considerable amount of aggravation was expressed as a large number of coffees were evidently spilled over their respective skippers.

There now remained just two last jobs before the big off. The effect of the wind needed to be taken into account. Given that the formation would be flying in an easterly direction and that the wind was coming from the south at four knots, it would blow them to the left of their track; and unless allowed for, they would pass to the north of Hoghton Tower. Using his navigator's computer, Captain Cumulus established that the wind would cause them to drift seven degrees to the left of their track, and hence to make their track good they would need to use a heading seven degrees further to the right. That meant that instead of using a heading of 102°M to get to their destination, they must use a heading of 109ºM. The last calculation had been completed.

It was now 1200 hours, and in eighteen minutes the Great Cloud Parade would commence. Captains gave out instructions to test the special effects: drizzle by wave two, and thunder and coloured lightning followed by a downpour by wave three. All went well, and then it was time to lower the Union Jack flag below the *Nimbus*.

With five minutes to go, Puffy was ordered to contact Warton Aerodrome to gain clearance to fly through their control zone. As he did that, the captain issued his last instruction to the formation. "This is your captain speaking. At exactly 1218 hours, we will start the run in for our Great Cloud Parade. Each one of you must maintain your position in the formation accurately, and whilst I have the responsibility of leading you to our target, you all have a responsibility to maintain a heading of 109° magnetic and a height of 1,300 feet whilst also maintaining an indicated airspeed of twenty knots. Remember that it is the queen taking the salute, and it is our duty to get it right. Once we have crossed over the top of Hoghton Tower, I will give the order to break formation, and each of you can make your own way back to Wythenshawe Weather Centre. On the approach to the tower, I will give the instructions for the special effects. Good luck to each and every one of you!"

In the last few minutes before the start of the flypast, there was complete silence in each of the thirty-nine Cloud Machines. The atmosphere in each was electric; each crew member was feeling a combination of anxiety, excitement, and pride that they were taking part in such a unique event that would surely go down in history. This last thought had not escaped Captain Cumulus, who in a moment of vanity was anticipating a reward: a CDM, perhaps!

They Are Off

By looking straight ahead using the TV camera on board the *Nimbus*, the Captain could see the River Ribble coursing through the gap between Salter's Bank on the port side and Long Bank to starboard. Lytham St Anne's and the Blackpool coastline stretched out further to port, whilst further out to starboard one could see Southport. There was a slight haze about, but on the whole visibility was good. The Bowland Hills, some forty nautical miles away, stood out quite well.

At 1217 hours there was one minute to go! With one hand on the throttle and the other holding the radio microphone, Captain Cumulus counted down the seconds. With fifteen to go he announced, "Parade, stand by, fifteen to go." Then he gave the countdown. "Ten, nine, eight, seven, six, five, four, three, two, one. Parade, go!" The Cloud Machines set in motion at precisely 1218 hours, and the whole choreographed formation set off in majestic style on the final stage of the operation.

Whilst the world-famous Leyland Band entertained the throng at Hoghton Tower and children pestered their parents for ice cream, the great formation of clouds made its way towards the Ribble estuary. After some eighteen minutes they were overhead the estuary at a point opposite Lytham St Anne's.

The next thirty-three minutes were spent flying inland, down the estuary to the first way mark where the River Douglas flowed into the Ribble. As the formation made its way to this first way mark, it passed Warton Aerodrome on its port side. The workers in the big aircraft factory at Warton had been informed about the Great Cloud Parade when the captain had first filed his flight plan, and his engineer Puffy White had asked for clearance to fly through their control zone. Now the worker's filed out onto the airfield in their thousands to wave and cheer at the great spectacle. This round of cheers brought a great deal of satisfaction to the thirty-nine crews and raised their level of expectancy regarding the reception that might be waiting for them at Hoghton Tower. In spite of the crews not being visible to the outside world, it did not stop some of them from waving back at their TV screens.

It was 1309 hours, and the formation left the Ribble estuary, which curved away to the left, leaving them over land as they continued east-south-east on a heading of 109 degrees magnetic. Some eighteens minutes later, the police headquarters at Hutton passed directly under the *Nimbus,* and a mischievous Captain Cumulus immediately issued an instruction. "Wave three, number thirteen, open up a downpour." Because the great cloud formation stretched out over a distance of three nautical miles, it was nine minutes later that the Hutton police HQ got a direct hit. It was not planned deliberately that it should coincide with a passing out parade for the latest qualifying recruits, but that didn't stop a wry smile from appearing on the captain's face, and Puffy had a great chuckle.

Twelve minutes later, at exactly 1348 hours, the *Nimbus* was overhead junction 30, with four nautical miles to go and twelve minutes left to reach the target, Hoghton Tower. They were going to do it!

The crowd of people at the Tower got their first real view of the Great Cloud Parade as the formation reached the motorway junction. The noise started to diminish as awe began to set in ahead of the impending flypast. The queen also started to look down the long entrance drive in a westerly direction from which the cloud formation was approaching. They both appeared to be at the same height at this point, and Her Majesty needed a little reassurance that indeed they were not—or were they?

At this point the crowd could not make out the nature of the formation; all they could see approaching was a line of swan-like Westmorland whites with no gaps between them visible, but that panorama would change as the *Nimbus* progressed ever nearer.

Shortly after junction 30 had been left behind, the first calamity occurred. Puffy White accidently knocked the winch control that wound up and down the cable that had attached to it the weighted Union Jack flag, which now started to unwind towards the earth. Upon reaching its full extremity, the flag was only a few feet above ground, and before anyone noticed and before anything could be done, it neatly hooked a rather large pair of ladies' blue bloomers from a washing line behind a house on the outskirts of a place called Gregson Lane. The blue-coloured bloomers wrapped themselves around the Union Jack, largely obscuring it.

Captain Cumulus was made aware of the drama by a radio call from one of the other machines in wave one, and a short but curt instruction involving some coloured language was immediately issued to Puffy, who at once reset the winch control to commence rewinding. With the aid of others in the formation, Puffy was able to reposition the flag in its approximate place below the *Nimbus,* but what he couldn't do was shake off the pair of blue ladies' bloomers.

Nine minutes after the *Nimbus* had passed over junction 30, at 1357 hours and with one nautical mile to go, the crowd at Hoghton Tower could see the arrowhead that wave one was formed into but could not make out the gaps between them or the details of what was suspended below the *Nimbus.* The trailing edge of row three in wave three was just overhead the motorway junction at this point.

For the next three final minutes, the *Nimbus* led the Great Cloud Parade slowly and serenely onward to Hoghton Tower, flying down the centre of the long drive that led up to the Tower itself and Her Majesty the Queen. The full detail of the arrowhead formation was now obvious to everyone as the nine machines in wave one filled the overhead vision of every observer, and the sight of these wonderful pearly white, swan-like Westmorland White clouds was truly amazing. The oohs and aahs were followed initially by clapping and cheering, but that changed to a great outburst of laughter as people saw the blue ladies' bloomers, fluttering in a less than flattering manner below the lead machine.

"Whatever will the queen make of it?" was the question doing the rounds amongst the populace gathered for this splendid occasion. In reality the queen was amused but did not give the fact away, thinking it more appropriate to appear displeased. Other dignitaries present were quick to announce their displeasure, but Captain Cumulus, standing to attention in front of his cockpit console, sailed on in bliss, completely ignorant of his association with blue bloomers.

It took a full three minutes for wave one to pass over Hoghton Tower, and as it did so the sky darkened as the three columns of less tidy-looking Cumberland Greys reached the start of the long drive. Captain Cumulus issued an instruction to the last machines in each of the outer columns, numbers five and fifteen, to start the drizzle. Whilst angel rays were not so obvious, pretty rainbows were evident, and a fresh set of oohs and aahs accompanied the fifteen machines making their way overhead.

Throughout the passage of waves one and two, Leyland's world-famous band played music appropriate to this grand occasion. Kenneth Alfords "On the Quarterdeck" had accompanied wave one, and wave two had been heralded by "A Life on the Ocean Wave" by H. Russel, but the mood was to change as wave three approached.

The sky darkened considerably as the first row of Manchester Blacks arrived behind wave two: five huge, menacing black beasts extending hundreds of feet upwards before forming the anvil shape of true storm clouds. The width of each row was considerable and extended out a significant distance to either side of Hoghton Tower. The mood was enhanced by the band playing Howard Snells' arrangement of Respighi's "The Pines of Rome", which musically paints the picture of a returning victorious Roman army stamping its feet louder and louder as it gets nearer. Everyone watched in awe as the menacing formation flew on in what seemed like a never-ending procession, and Her Majesty was most impressed until catastrophe struck.

Just as the second row of Manchester Blacks reached the start of the long drive, the captains of the two outer clouds responded to the order, "Lightning and thunder on." The fan duct motors on the starboard outer machine—number ten, to be exact—lost a degree of power, and its skipper, an Italian by the name of Albertino Insomnio, suffered the acute embarrassment of watching the rest of the formation leaving him trailing behind. The knock-on effect of this was that the cloud immediately behind him, number fifteen in the wave, had to slow down as well to keep station with Albertino. This problem was further compounded when Albertino's machine, which went by the name *Astro*, created its first bolt of red lightning. The fan duct motors jammed in a position that sent it heading north-north-east, which would, if not corrected, take it diagonally overhead Hoghton Tower. The machine following *Astro* had to keep station and consequently followed whilst delivering the downpour ordered by Captain Cumulus.

Whilst this drama was unfolding, the other thirty-seven machines continued onwards, and Her Majesty and her loyal subjects were most impressed as the first wide row of five Manchester Blacks passed overhead, to be followed by a row of four with the one on the right, creating bolts of red, white, and blue lightning followed by loud claps of thunder, all of which was fairly scary but safe because this particular cloud was well outside the boundary of Hoghton Tower. The third row of four was in perfect position behind the second, and the cloud on the outer right provided a heavy downpour and a spectacular angel ray without a drop falling on anyone in the Tower grounds.

As the last of wave three passed over Hoghton Tower, the remaining two clouds, numbers ten and fifteen, could be observed travelling from the left and across the flight path of their colleagues, heading frighteningly towards the Tower itself. Leyland Band stopped playing, and their instruments were left where they had been played as the musicians headed for whatever cover they could find. They were not the only ones in apparent panic.

The *Astro* gave one final bolt of blue lightning just before reaching the Tower, but unfortunately it struck one of the band's tubas, which shot into the air before dropping on to one of the bass drums, puncturing it and denting the Tuba beyond repair. The queen, most uncharacteristically, tried to take cover by moving to a side of the tower that obscured the oncoming bolts of lightning, but that gave her no warning of the approach of the final cloud, a remnant from row three that was by now subjecting everyone that it passed over to a complete drenching. Her Majesty was not spared.

There was an eerie silence at Hoghton Tower after the last cloud left the scene. The folks that had come to witness the spectacle could see that the queen was greatly distressed, and most decided that it would be prudent to depart silently. The main concern of the Leyland Band, however, was the damage caused and the cost of replacements, which they estimated would be in the region of ten thousand pounds.

The Aftermath

Captain Cumulus checked his watch: 1415 hours. The last clouds in the formation should have cleared Hoghton Tower six minutes ago, and it was time to break up the formation and instruct everyone to make their way back to Wythenshawe Weather Centre. The captain duly gave the instruction and complimented them all on a job well done, because he had no knowledge that would lead him to feel anything else. Indeed, he had visions of Her Majesty pinning on him a CDM sometime in the future. A suitable portrait would not be out of place in his home, and to celebrate his success right now, he ordered Puffy to open the jug marked "Rob's Tea".

The Captain of the *Astro*, Albertino Insomnio, continued on a north-north-east heading, over which he had little control. The southerly wind was now a tail wind, and so he had only one course of action open to him: to descend to ground level as soon as possible and see what the problem was. The question was where. Lucky for him, Salmesbury Aerodrome lay across the path he was taking, and in due course he landed there.

To Albertino's surprise, the machine that had been behind him, the *Discovery,* had also landed. Its skipper, Wally Lenticular, a tall, thin character, joined him to discuss what had happened. A quick inspection of the fan duct motors on the *Astro* revealed that two motors had failed, which had caused it to slow down, and a bolt of lightning had welded the motors into a position that forced it to alter course. After the two captains discussed things, the *Discovery* headed back to the Wythenshawe Weather Centre whilst engineers from Black, Black & Blackemore's were called in to repair the *Astro,* which would remain at Salmesbury for a few days.

Upon arrival at the Wythenshawe Weather Centre, the Captain was a little surprised to find that only thirty-seven machines had made it back, but he was reassured when his fellow captains pointed out that they had probably landed somewhere to sort out a technical problem. Cirrus Cumulus and Puffy White headed for home feeling very satisfied with themselves.

During the course of the next few days, news reached Captain Cumulus that the two missing Cloud Machines had indeed returned, and for the moment that was the end of the whole business. However, on June 16 the post arrived as usual, and Puffy brought it to the captain. One of the envelopes in Puffy's hand was marked OHMS, or "On Her Majesty's Service", and in a moment of sheer excitement Cirrus Cumulus tore open the envelope, fully expecting that it was to inform him of his impending decoration by the Queen at the Palace. This feeling was rapidly displaced by one of incredulity as he read the contents.

Her Majesty the Queen has instructed her Government to convene a board of inquiry.

The board of inquiry is to fully investigate the role of Captain C. Cumulus in the disastrous Great Cloud Parade, held on June 2 at Hoghton Tower. The inquiry will be held at Wythenshawe Weather Centre on June 20, at 10.00 am sharp, and Captain Cirrus Cumulus is hereby instructed to attend.

Signed,
Superintendant I. N. Spite, CDM

It was a dismal ending to what should have been a good day, and now the captain had to contemplate what it was all about and what could potentially happen to him—but that's another story.

WHERE HAVE ALL THE CLOUDS GONE?

Hiding Away

Captain Cumulus was still feeling hurt after the reprimand he had recently received, and he decided to make the journey to his second home in Ballyhalbert, to regain his composure and re-establish his dignity amongst people that were unlikely to be aware of his downfall. Faithful engineer Puffy White accompanied the captain to Ballyhalbert, which was a lovely, unspoilt village on the Irish Sea coast on the Ards Peninsula. Here they would have the best of all worlds to recuperate: the sea, the countryside, and friendly people.

The board of inquiry set up to investigate the role of Captain C. Cumulus in the disastrous Great Cloud Parade had left a scar on the mind of the captain. The interrogation he had undergone at Wythenshawe Weather Centre was something he had never experienced before, and he certainly never wanted to again. The inquiry had been rigorous and covered all aspects of the operation. True, the board had concluded that the mishap which resulted in Her Majesty the Queen getting drenched was the result of an unfortunate malfunction onboard the Cloud Machine *Astro,* for which Captain Cumulus could not be held responsible, but because he had the overall responsibility for the operation, he ought to have had a contingency plan, and in this respect he had failed.

Fortunately, the captain had got off fairly lightly with three endorsement points on his Cloud Machine licence, which up to this point had been clean. His comprehensive insurance cover would probably go up in cost now, but on the whole it could have been worse. He would have to be extra careful in future in order to avoid any further endorsements. If he got six, he could be suspended, just like Abigail Windrush, skipper of the *Hurricane*. Abigail was suspended for twelve months after getting six endorsement points; the first three were awarded for flying below the cloud base in daylight and in the opposite direction to all the natural clouds above the town of Aberystwyth, which resulted in a huge number of telephone calls to the police from members of the public in panic mode who had witnessed this unnatural phenomenon. This was a gross infringement of the rules laid down in the *Cloud Machine Operators Rules of Operation Manual,* which clearly stated that whenever it was necessary to journey in the opposite direction to natural clouds, it must be done under the cover of darkness or above the cloud base of a sky covered by stratus clouds.

Abigail gained her next three endorsement points in a most bizarre fashion. She had been doing a job in the Faroe Islands and was heading back home in a southerly direction, on a heading that would see her flying down the Isle-of-Lewis in the Outer Hebrides. It was on a cloudless Sunday afternoon, and Abigail wanted to get home before the pubs closed, so she needed to step on it. She had a thirty-knot tail wind, and when she fully opened the *Hurricane*'s throttles, she was rattling along at sixty knots. Now, as the only cloud in the sky, it would look rather peculiar to be skimming across the heavens. In order not scare anyone, she dropped down to the height of the roadside telephone poles, where she would be less conspicuous.

To lighten her load a little, she decided to make rain as she travelled down the island. All this was fine, but because it was Sunday, the island's residents were taking advantage of the good weather. A group of cyclists from The Stornaway and Comeback Wayfarers' Club were making their way home to Stornaway in a southerly direction along the only road on the island that linked Point-of-Ness with the island's capital. The group, sharing the same tailwind as the *Hurricane*, were moving along steadily at about twenty miles an hour.

"Thars a great clood catching us up fro' behind," cried the rear-most rider.

"Rubbish, thars nae a clood in the sky," came the reply from the front.

Before anyone could call, "Up your kilt," the speedy cyclists were being overtaken by an even speedier low cloud that was bringing a rain storm with it. The first the group really knew of its immediate approach was when they were embraced by the dark shadow that preceded it, and the sudden loss of light was quickly followed by a rush of wind and a torrential downpour. It was all over in no time, and the group came to a sudden halt as they watched the cloud hurtle down the road almost at ground level, belching rain as it went.

Among the more repeatable remarks were, "That should not be allowed."

"Aye, it's bloody dangerous."

"Mah knickers are soaked."

"I'll dry 'em for yea."

"You'll no' touch mah knickers."

The group of cyclists made a formal complaint, which along with several others resulted in Abigail Windrush appearing in court. The charges brought were twofold: first, that Windrush had exceeded the speed limit laid down in the *Cloud Machine Operators Rules of Operation Manual*, which gave a maximum of thirty knots; and second, dangerous low flying and grievous bodily soaking. It was a clear-cut case of wind rush by name and wind rush by nature!

Back to Reality

A letter dropped through the letter box, and Puffy picked it up. It seemed to Puffy that the letter was rather important because it had a solicitor's logo on the envelope.

"Letter just come for you, Captain."

"Let's have look, then, shall we?"

Puffy half expected it to contain Captain Cumulus's Cloud Machine licence, with the endorsement points added.

"Damn and blast, it just keeps on getting worse!" exclaimed the captain.

"What's up?" asked Puffy.

"Leyland Band has made a claim against me."

"Whatever for?"

"They claim I am responsible for damaging a tuba and a bass drum."

"What have you got to do, then?" asked Puffy.

"They claim it will cost ten thousand pounds to buy new instruments, and I haven't got that kind of money to spare," replied the captain.

"Will your insurance not cover it, Captain?"

"It will, but I will lose my no-claims bonus, and that will bump up my next premium payment," replied a despondent captain. "Right, Puffy, we can't go on doing nothing here in Ballyhalbert anymore. We need to get back to work and earn some cash, even if that means facing the ridicule of my colleagues."

That's determination for you, thought Puffy, who was most impressed with his captain's attitude. It was all very well being here in Northern Ireland enjoying the peace and tranquillity, but it would not stop the world going round, and he—that is to say, the captain—needed to face his colleagues and friends at some point and move on.

"Get some tickets on the next ferry to Liverpool, Puffy. We are going to get back to business."

"Aye aye, Captain."

The voyage to Liverpool was an enjoyable experience. Once the ship left Belfast Lough, it headed south-east with the Ards Peninsula on the starboard side, and soon the Isle of Man came into view on the port side. Captain Cumulus spent some time musing on what kind of a reception he was going to get when he ultimately arrived at the Wythenshawe Weather Centre. No doubt he would be the butt of his colleagues' jokes, but that was something with which he would have to cope.

It was a short journey from Liverpool to home, and the following day the captain and his faithful engineer made their way apprehensively to Wythenshawe Weather Centre, where their Cloud Machine, the *Nimbus,* had been left hangared whilst they had taken a sojourn in Northern Ireland.

On arrival at the Weather Centre, they both entered the huge hangar, which usually housed a considerable number of Cloud Machines, but they were somewhat taken aback by the sight that confronted them. Only two Cloud Machines appeared to be present, the *Nimbus* and the *Discovery,* and in the case of the latter, its skipper, Wally Lenticular, was busy working on it.

Puffy and Captain Cumulus strode over to the *Discovery*. "Wally, where have all the clouds gone?" asked the captain.

"Where have you been hiding yourself, Cirrus?" retorted Wally. Before the captain could answer, he went on. "They are working for Eddie Stormbart these days. He has a contract off the government."

"But Eddie Stormbart has a fleet of his own Cloud Machines," noted Puffy.

"That might be, but this is a big contract, a real big job."

"So what's the job, then?"

"Its foreign aid see," said Wally. "They take rain to drought-ridden foreign climes, hundreds of 'em at a time." Wally's animated face went on to describe how it was all organised. Hundreds of Cloud Machines would head out in the dark to an agreed location over the Atlantic Ocean and atomise millions of gallons of the sea. Then they would form up into a mammoth cloud convoy before making their slow way to wherever they were required to provide rain. When the job was done, it would be repeated time and time again until they were told otherwise. "Them clever professor blokes reckon it'll stop the melting ice caps from raising the level of the oceans. Well, it makes sense, don't it? The ice melts, you get more sea, but along comes Eddie Stormbart and his mob, and they atomise it all and chuck it on a desert. Clever, isn't it? He should get a gong for that. And talking about gongs, Cirrus . . ."

But before Wally could continue, the captain butted in. "How come you're not working for Eddie?"

"I was, but the *Discovery* needed an MOT, and here I am," he replied.

"How's the foreign aid job going?" inquired Puffy.

"Pretty well in general. They have had some hiccups, or maybe I should say stormcups. One of the convoys heading for Morocco got blown off course, and they had to lighten their loads in the usual way. It just so happened that they were passing over the Azores at the time, and it caused horrible flooding, but there you are. There's a risk with everything. You could sign on with Eddie—he still needs more help."

"What do you think, Cirrus?" said Puffy.

"Its Captain Cumulus to you," said the captain, who then went on to say in a gruff voice. "We'll make our way to the office and see what the score is."

"Did you hear about Windy Blower, the skipper of the *Spitting*?" asked Wally.

"No. What about him?"

"He got a scam goin', see. He thought he could undercut Eddie Stormbart. He got this idea that it was a waste of time ploughing all them nautical miles over the Atlantic to atomise the sea. He thought he could cut that long journey out by atomising the water on the mainland. It worked at first. He bloomin' well dried up the Leeds-Liverpool canal and the Manchester Ship Canal, and he nearly got away with it, but he went too far, see."

"What happened?"

"Well, it was like this. It was on a Monday morning, and all the good folk living in their big houses and little uns, around the shores of Lake Windermere, woke up and looked through their windows. They could see that the lake had gone. Well, you could imagine it, they all wondered where Lake Windermere had disappeared to, and then they got angry. "Look at my two masted schooner scuppered on the bottoms" exclaimed one of the locals. Boats were very popular in a place like Windermere, so imagine a whole valley of sludge where once before there had been a huge stretch of water with ferry boats and yachts of all shapes and sizes bobbing up and down on it, not to mention the wide variety of birds. No, sludge was not going to be well received as an alternative.

"Well, go on," cried Puffy, fascinated by this tale of woe.

"The authorities investigated, and it didn't take 'em long to discover what had happened and who were involved, it bein' connected with a government job."

The captain asked, "Windy couldn't have done it on his own?"

"No, Cirrus, you're right. He had about fifty mates helping, and they had it empty in a night. Just imagine, a lake there at night and gone the following morning. It must have been a shock."

"What happened to Windy?" asked the captain.

"He and all is mates lost their licences, and that's why Eddie Stormbart's lookin' for help."

Captain Cumulus turned to Puffy and announced that they would make their way immediately to the Weather Centre Office, but just as they were about to depart, Wally posed a final question. "Would you like to take part in a sponsored wee?"

A hurried departure followed, demonstrating a distinct lack of enthusiastic support, but at least they knew where all the clouds had gone.

HOW DO YOU FILL AN EMPTY LAKE?

The Aftermath

What an unsightly thing Lake Windermere had become. From a scene of tranquillity to a valley of mud, and all in the duration of an evening! It was a shock for all those living around the lake to wake up in the morning and be greeted by an empty lake. The local police were inundated with callers inquiring about the "stolen" lake. If they knew it was on its way to the Middle East as part of the government's foreign aid programme, it was doubtful that they would be placated. The truth of the matter was that the local constabulary had no idea what had happened to the lake, and the desk sergeant in the Windermere office was doubtful about its disappearance before he saw it himself, preferring to think that the local pubs had done a roaring trade the night before.

A valley of mud was not something that anyone would choose to have on his doorstep, and the locals lost no time in complaining to their local councillors and their MP, but they were initially at a loss as to what to do. None of them had any experience of losing a lake, and for once they had little to say on the matter other than they would make inquiries.

The loss of Lake Windermere posed a number of problems relating both to the local economy and transport. An important car ferry connected Windermere to Hawkshead, and locals commuted by it for work. The alternative was a long and expensive road journey that lengthened the working day considerably. A number of local companies depended on the lake for business connected with tourism, and they would be hit particularly badly, especially the ferry that ran during the summer from the northern end to the southern, carrying thousands of holidaymakers. The lake was also host to a number of sailing clubs whose activities had come to a halt. Whoever had stolen this lake had a lot to answer for and many people to answer to. The one saving grace over the coming days was the influx of sightseers who thronged to the locality to witness the panorama, but they were not destined to continue making the journey for any great length of time.

The valley of mud played host to a variety of debris and dead fish. It was sad to see what had happened to Windermere's fish stock, but it represented Christmas to the many fish-eating birds, and word got round mightily fast with the result that thousands of birds, the majority being seagulls, were swarming over the area to take advantage of the feast flickering helplessly in the mud. The birds brought with them their own problems, namely bird droppings, which fell in great quantities on the locality and to such an extent that the locals could only venture out safely with an umbrella. As for those contemplating putting washing on a line, well, they could forget it. The lake's secrets were also revealed and took on a number of forms. One of the first things anyone would spot amongst the debris was the large number of prams which took most people by surprise, and one had to wonder where all the mothers were.

Judging by some of the corpses on view, the police would have a field day resolving outstanding cases of murder, suicide, and accidental deaths, although how they would do that was a conundrum for most people. The greatest revelation of all, however, was an RAF Sunderland flying boat from the Second World War. These aircraft had been assembled in a plant in White Cross Bay during the war, but there was no record of one being sunk. Clearly a number of museums would be interested in salvaging this historical aircraft.

One of the more unpleasant side effects of the missing lake was the aroma that started to ferment as the day moved on. There was a lot to rot in the exposed mud, and with the heat of the mid-day sun, rot it started to do and to a point where the word "aroma" did it unfair justice; stench being a more tale-telling title. The stench was a fatal attraction for the insect world, who, now fully alerted, were making their way to the scene in droves, headed by swarms of Gestapo-looking bluebottles. Windermere was becoming a different place, and those people who'd made a second home here started doubting the wisdom of their investments.

New but not enchanting sounds emanated from the mud ensemble that had replaced the serene lake. Oozes, plops, and other strange sounds could be heard, accompanied by the chorus of birds in an erratic overture lacking in any melodic quality. The baying of the fly-inflicted local cow's choir had a tendency to introduce its own contribution, but not in any co-ordinated fashion. The real coup de grace, was a sound that could only be described by asking one to think about a wellington boot being extricated painfully slowly from deep, soft mud that only gives things up after an intense struggle. This latter sound was created by those brave individuals who waded out to their cherished boats sitting in the mud close to the shore line.

Many paintings and photographs of Lake Windermere adorn a multitude of walls in a multitude of places, extolling its natural beauty, and they are evidence of the attraction of the place for painters and photographers. The current rearrangement of things proved a new attraction for photographers but less so for painters, who tend to need more aesthetically pleasing vistas before committing to canvas. Although photographing the situation for posterity had its virtues, it was unlikely that their publication would help to promote it as a tourist attraction, and picture postcards would most definitely be off the agenda.

How Did It Happen?

The question that everyone was asking was, "How did it happen?" For the moment no one had an answer. Local councillors hurriedly convened a meeting with the water authorities, the police, and lake users to begin an investigation. There was much scratching of heads and clearing of throats as a hundred or so minds concentrated on finding an answer to the question on everyone's lips, but it was not easy. There was no plug hole at the bottom of Lake Windermere—or was there? A helicopter flight scoured the muddy valley but found no evidence of a plug hole. What else could it be?

Local councillor Fred Wainwright, in a moment of inspiration, piped up. "There's a bloke lives next to me that has a Cloud Machine, and he atomises water to make clouds to take to various places and make rain. Maybe something like that has happened."

"Who's the bloke?" someone asked.

"I think they call him Windy Blower."

The meeting was brought to a close, with the police being instructed to make inquiries.

It didn't take long for the police to establish that Windy Blower and some fifty other Cloud Machine owners working for Eddie Stormbart had been working a scam and had stolen Lake Windermere. The police exonerated both Eddie Stormbart and Wythenshawe Weather Centre, whom Windy and his accomplices had been working for on a government contract, from any involvement. In due course a court case was held in Lancaster which made headline reading in the national press:

Cloud Machines used to Steal Lake Windermere

Lancaster attracted huge crowds on the day of the court case, and there was much booing and hissing as Windy and others came before the judge. Each defendant lost his or her Cloud Machine licences and was banned for five years from flying. As further punishment, each had to perform a year's community service clearing debris from the muddy valley that was Lake Windermere, but that proved difficult when the lake was refilled.

Matters now moved on in the Lake District, to the question of who would pay for the muddy valley to be filled up again with water—and not just any water, because the lake previously held three-star-rated stuff. Most locals expressed the view that claims should be lodged with the Cloud Machine owners' insurers, and they initiated this process. A negative response came back: the insurers explained that their policies did not extend to covering illegal activities, and because the owners had been found guilty in court, they had no obligation to pay anything out. Fortunately, the Guild of Cloud Machine Owners had a fund into which all owners paid, and on being informed of the dastardly deed, it came to the rescue with the necessary finance even though at this stage the cost was not known.

Attention now turned to filling up the lake. How could it be done? Filling it with buckets was certainly out of the question, as was a sponsored pee, which would not only upset the local female population but would also result in a lake full of toxic fluid that would prevent fish life and many other forms of life from re-establishing themselves; swimming might also be a dodgy pastime in a lake of pee water. Whatever the solution, it had to be on a big scale. The only obvious choice to spring to mind was the use of tankers to bring water in from a relevant source, and here the three-star grading came to the forefront once more. Using tankers would take time, and they would not benefit the area as a tourist attraction.

"What about using Cloud Machines? If they can empty a lake, they can fill one," was an opinion expressed at a planning meeting, and so it came to be.

The job would be advertised in the normal way at Wythenshawe Weather Centre.

Captain Cumulus and his engineer, Puffy White, were busy scanning the jobs on offer board at the Weather Centre when they came across the Lake Windermere job. The card read:

Due to unforeseen circumstances,
Lake Windermere is currently empty.

Applications are invited from Cloud Machine owners to apply to fill it. Lake Windermere holds three-star-rated water, and a suitable source must be located by the applicant. A period of three months has been allocated to refilling the lake. A penalty will be imposed for each day after the three months have elapsed.

Fee to be negotiated.

Applications to: Keswick Borough Surveyor,
Water Street,
Keswick
H20 C02

Puffy recognised a smile on the captain's face and was well pleased. This would get them back into work and avoid the humdrum convoys associated with working for Eddie Stormbart. More important, with some revenue coming in, the bill for Leyland Band's instruments may be affordable without making any excessive claims on the *Nimbus* insurance policy.

"Puffy, go and ask the office for an application form. I think we will have a go at this."

"Aye aye, Captain."

Formulating a Plan

It was obvious to Captain Cumulus that if he was to stand a good chance of being considered for the job, he'd better have a good plan, and so he started to give the task some serious consideration before completing the application form. The first thing that crossed his mind was the fact that not any old water would do. Lake Windermere had been full of three-star-rated stuff, and that meant that he couldn't just nip out over the Irish Sea and bring some of it to Windermere; there was no comparison between brine and three-star water.

Some consideration would have to be given to locating sources of three-star-rated water, and that may not be so easy. Fortunately, a conversation with Puffy revealed that a catalogue of water sources by grades existed, and a copy was held at Wythenshawe Weather Centre. Puffy had, however, completely forgotten that there was a reference book onboard the *Nimbus,* but then again he was prone to forgetfulness.

"Puffy, nip down to the Weather Centre, will you, and borrow a copy of the *Weather Sources Catalogue*. I'm going to need to consult it."

"Aye aye, Captain." Then he thought, *Another bloomin' errand to run.* But it was gratifying that his captain was seriously trying to get work. Puffy didn't wish to contemplate redundancy. He still hadn't remembered the copy kept onboard the *Nimbus*.

Whilst Puffy was making the journey to Wythenshawe, the captain started to ponder the problem of how much water would be needed to fill Lake Windermere. *Maybe details will be in the catalogue,* he thought, but a little research of his flying charts would not go amiss. He established from his charts that Windermere was 11.25 miles long and 0.93 miles wide at its widest point. The lake was 219 feet deep at one point. However, he could find no details of the number of gallons of water that it held. The catalogue that Puffy returned with didn't provide the information, either; it simply listed sources of water under their respective grading. At least the captain could make a list of three-star-rated sources to consider.

Once the captain had made a list of the appropriate sources, he looked in detail at the length, width, and depth of each one. It was possible that the solution may be to take some water from several sources to do the job, although that was not the ideal solution. On the other hand, to fill Windermere may take the emptying of another lake or reservoir, which would be a bit like robbing Peter to pay Paul.

"How much water do you need, Captain?" inquired Puffy.

"Well, I know that Lake Windermere was emptied in one night, and it took fifty Cloud Machines to do it. Each one carried the maximum they could atomise, and each one did one trip to complete the job."

"So if you do fifty trips to some place, you could do the job?"

"That's right, Puffy, and if we did five a week, then it could be finished in ten weeks, with weekends off and two weeks to spare for any unforeseen eventualities."

"I wouldn't like to live in Windermere for them ten weeks," remarked Puffy.

"Why not?"

"It will be raining every day."

"We'll fill it up at night, and their weekends will be unaffected."

"That's great, Captain: you have a plan!"

"No, I don't—not yet, anyway. I need to find out from where I can take the water."

Captain Cumulus arranged a meeting with the superintendant at Wythenshawe Weather Centre, Mr I. N. Spite, CDM, to discuss the delicate issue of where the water for Windermere could be taken from.

"Have you anywhere in mind?" asked Mr Spite.

"Loch Ness has a lot to commend it," answered Captain Cumulus. "Loch Ness is 23 miles long, 1.7 miles wide at its widest point, and 755 feet deep at its deepest. I could take all I needed from this one source, and it would still be two-thirds full. What worries me is that it is part of a hydro-electric scheme that generates a lot of electricity, and I don't want to interfere with that."

Mr Spite could see the wisdom and dilemma of the plan and mused a little before commenting, "I think I remember that the hydro-electric plant was to be shut down for a period of maintenance. Now, if that could be co-ordinated with your job, your plan could be a goer."

With that, Mr Spite left the room to make some inquiries. He returned thirty minutes later with the news that Cumulus could go ahead and take some of the Loch Ness water. The hydro-electric plant was due to go offline for six months, and that would be ample time for the Loch to replenish itself from a combination of rain and water rolling down off the hillsides. As an unexpected bonus, this would be a wonderful opportunity for all those Loch Ness Monster fans to perform some additional research as the loch's level fell.

Captain Cumulus and Puffy were ecstatic even though they hadn't yet been hired to do the job.

Mr. Spite said, "What about a back up machine? You will need one just in case your *Nimbus* breaks down."

"That's a good point, Mr Spite. I will have to arrange that. Thanks for mentioning it."

"Well, get off and make that application. I think you stand a good chance!"

The *Discovery* should have completed its MOT by now, and Captain Cumulus decided to give its owner, Wally Lenticular, a call. "Hello, Wally, it's Cirrus here."

He must be after something, thought Wally. *He doesn't normally use his first name when he introduces himself.* "What can I do for you, Cirrus?"

Slightly cringing at someone using his first name, Captain Cumulus went through the rigmarole of telling Wally about the job for which he wanted to apply.

"What are you telling me for, Cirrus?"

Another cringe followed before he replied, "I need someone to act as a reserve, just in case the *Nimbus* breaks down. Will you be my reserve?"

"What's in it for me? If I'm reserve for you, I can't take on any work for three months."

"I'll pay you a retainer fee if I get the job, Wally."

A fee was negotiated and the deal was done. The captain was now in a position to complete and submit his application form.

Puffy was delighted to be posting such an important letter to the Keswick Borough Surveyor.

In due course, Captain Cumulus was invited to attend an interview in the Town Hall at Keswick. and on arrival he had only a short while to wait before being ushered into the Borough Surveyor's Office. Samuel Humbug was a stern, no-nonsense character, and his presence was somewhat off-putting. Nevertheless, Cirrus Cumulus sat down and waited for the impending questions. He couldn't afford to do otherwise—the job was too important to him. Mr Humbug pored over the application form and then lifted his head to reveal a large port wine-coloured nose before commenting forcefully, "This is a very detailed plan that you have submitted, and you are to be commended for your thoroughness. When can you start, Mr Cumulus?"

The captain was taken aback by the rapidity of the surveyor's decision, and he was irritated at the same time for not being addressed as he thought fit.

"I can start at your earliest convenience, but—"

He got no further than that before Mr Humbug interjected. "Good! We can sort out the remuneration details, and my secretary will forward them on to you along with a start date. Now, I'm very busy, so please see you yourself out." And with that the interview was concluded.

When the captain got outside the Town Hall and met Puffy, all he could think of was a cup of tea.

"That was a short interview, Captain. I take it you were unsuccessful?"

"On the contrary, my dear Puffy. I've got the job, and that was the shortest interview in my life. Let's go and get a drink." And with that the two of them walked along the Keswick streets jauntily to find a suitable café.

The Mission

They still had to work out the final details of the task, and Captain Cumulus was kept busy for a few days putting the final touches to things. It was 180 nautical miles from Windermere to Loch Ness, and by travelling at the maximum speed allowed, which was thirty knots, it would take six hours to make the journey. The captain calculated that if he left Windermere at 3.00 pm, he would reach Loch Ness by 9.00 pm. He would allow one hour to atomise the water, and when fully fledged as a Manchester Black, he would start the departure from Scotland at 10.00 pm, arriving at Lake Windermere at 4.00 am the next day. He would create rain for one hour, and the *Nimbus* would dispense its cloud, minus the obligatory amount to mask itself, and be ready to leave the locality by 5.00 am. The work would be done whilst everyone was still in bed.

The job was going to mean long days, at least fourteen hours, and that was not taking into account from where the *Nimbus* would operate. Normally the *Nimbus* was hangared at the Wythenshawe Weather Centre, but it was unrealistic to start the mission from there because it would add too much journey time to Windermere and back at the start and finish of each day. Some alternative would have to be found. Fortunately Wally Lenticular came to the rescue. Wally had a pal that had an old hangar on the airfield at Cark, just south of the lake, and it was only twenty minutes' flying time to the start of the journey north to Loch Ness. Captain Cumulus made arrangements to hire the hangar for three months, and a caravan next to it would be home for Puffy and the Captain, although Puffy was none too keen on living in such close proximity to his boss. Finally everything was organised, the plan was finalised, and the mission was about to begin.

The *Nimbus* started its mission on a Monday in late September 2012. Captain Cumulus dialled Loch Ness into the navigation computer he had onboard, which went under the title "soakometer". This was a special piece of kit that enabled the *Nimbus* to be guided to particular water sources. There was no drama involved in the trips to Scotland. Each long day became routine, and by the weekend both the captain and his engineer felt pretty weary, but they were motivated by the fact that it was a good earner. There was no break in the routine, at least initially. After each flight, the

Nimbus topped up with the fuel that was required to run its four silent-running, fan duct motors. Wally had had the forethought to have a fuel bowser located at Cark airfield to top up the Cloud Machine as required. Wally was turning out to be a good ally.

Slowly but surely the water level at Loch Ness fell whilst water started to reappear at Lake Windermere. After three weeks there was a noticeable difference at both locations. The immediate benefit to the Lake District, and Windermere and Ambleside in particular, was both the change in view and the lowering in intensity of the stench, not to mention the decrease in bird noise and shit. The muddy valley was beginning to fill up with water, and the unsightly debris was disappearing. The source of food for the bird population diminished, and there appeared to be the start of a welcome migration, making it safe to step outdoors without an umbrella.

After six weeks the change at Windermere was marked to such a level that the ferries were able to start services again. Almost all the lake's boats were afloat now, and the various sailing clubs got back into business. Indeed, at this point there seemed little difference between the water level now and that a few years ago, when a severe drought had occurred.

During the eighth week of the mission, one of the fan duct motors on the *Nimbus* started to make strange noises, and there was a reduction in its power output. Puffy suggested to the Captain that the motor was in need of attention, and they made arrangements for engineers from Black, Black & Blakemore's in deeper Salford to come out and take a look at it. It became clear that the company's engineers would require a week to carry out repairs at Cark.

"Puffy, get in touch with Wally. He's going to have to take over for a week."

"Aye aye, Captain. I'll get on with it right away."

Wally brought the *Discovery* over to Cark and went over the mission plan with Cirrus.

"Now look, Wally, everything has been going on schedule for the last eight weeks, and I want the job finished in the next two. Are you happy with the plan, and are you confident that your machine is up to it?"

"Don't you worry, Cirrus, I'm up for the job, and so is the *Discovery*. It's not long since it had its MOT."

With that the temporary handover was completed.

The *Discovery* Takes Over

Wally had five trips to make to Loch Lomond, assuming the *Nimbus* would take no longer than a week to repair. Wally's Cloud Machine, the *Discovery*, had all the gadgets on board that the *Nimbus* had, although Wally was not as conversant with everything as Captain Cumulus. When it came to navigation, he preferred the "mark one eye ball" and his charts rather than rely on his soakometer. Nevertheless, everything got off to a good start, and he made three trouble-free journeys to Loch Ness and back to keep the topping-up process going. On the fourth trip it was a particularly dark night. It was a moonless period, and a high layer of stratus cloud blanked out any remaining night light, leaving an inky dark scenario of such magnitude that few ground features could be made out. Wally managed to navigate to Loch Ness, but for the journey back he would have to punch into the soakometer the co-ordinates of Lake Windermere and trust that it would be okay. If he remembered, he could check his position on his PPI, or plan position indicator. Wally decided to grab forty winks whilst the *Discovery* made its way back. The alarm went off at 3.30 am, just thirty minutes before the condensers on board should be switched on to make a heavy downpour for one hour. Wally couldn't see a thing on the TV screen mounted on the flight deck; the blackness prevented anything on the ground from being observed. At precisely 4.00 am Wally put the *Discovery* into a stationary hover and switched on the condensers. At 5.00 am Wally switched the condensers off again to stop the rain, and he made the short journey to Cark, which was aided by the early start of dawn. The arrival at Cark slightly mystified Wally. He was sure his approach was from a different direction than on the first three trips, but he didn't think to look at his PPI.

The final trip by the *Discovery* fared no better than the previous one regarding the light, and Wally was glad that this may be his last one. Everything went as it had the night before, but he had a sudden shock at 4.55 am as he was coming to the end of raining his load on what he thought was Lake Windermere. A casual glance at his PPI revealed that he was hovering over Wast Water, which was west of Windermere.

Bloody hell! thought Wally. *Either the soakometer is not calibrated correctly, or the wind has blown me off course.* It was too late to do anything now except return to Cark. *Crikey! I'm not going to say anything about this to Cirrus. He'll go nuts if he knows,* and that's where matters were left.

The *Nimbus* was repaired by the engineers from Black, Black & Blackemore's from deeper Salford whilst Wally was carrying out his five trips to Loch Ness, and Captain Cumulus was contemplating completing the job. "Well, Puffy, I reckon five final trips should do the job with two weeks to spare."

Sensing that his captain was in good spirits, Puffy had no intention of deflating things in any way, but he thought that it was too early to think that everything was done and dusted.

The captain cracked on with the last five flights only to find at the end of it that Lake Windermere was not fully topped up. "That's strange. I thought that fifty trips should do the trick."

"Aye, but you must remember, Cirrus, that when Windy Blower had his scam going, there were fifty-one Cloud Machines, if you include his own."

"It's Captain Cumulus to you, but you have got a point. We'll have to do an extra trip next week."

The *Nimbus* had to do two final trips to finish the job, which mystified the captain, but finish it he did, and Lake Windermere was restored to its former glory.

Job Done

A week later, a presentation was arranged in Windermere to, amongst other things, celebrate the refilling of the lake and to thank the crew of the *Nimbus* for performing a splendid job. Captain Cumulus took it upon himself to invite Wally Lenticular, but strangely he turned it down. The borough surveyor of Keswick, Mr Samuel Humbug, made the presentation, and Leyland Band provided some stunning music to raise the profile of the whole occasion. In Mr Humbug's inimitable style, he made a speech that was to the point and short, to say the least.

"Today we celebrate Lake Windermere's presence again, thanks to the job done by Captain Cumulus and his crew. We can also be thankful for the removal of the stench we have all suffered from lately and our bombardment from bird shit. As a bonus, several murders have been resolved, and a Sunderland flying boat was recovered."

"Pity he forgot to mention the flooding around Wast Water," mentioned a bystander.

After finishing his short speech, Mr Humbug stepped down from the temporarily erected stand and passed an envelope to the captain.

"That's the agreed fee, Mr Cumulus. Well done!"

With that the Keswick Borough surveyor rushed off, his assistant informing the captain that he had urgent business at Wasdale Head, where there had been some severe flooding.

Once the *Nimbus* had landed back in the hangar at Wythenshawe Weather Centre, the captain and Puffy made their way back home. Over a cup of tea, the captain opened the envelope and took out the cheque. The substantial sum that he had received would cover the cost of renting the facilities at Cark, pay for the fuel for the *Nimbus* and the retainer fee for Wally, and still there would be enough left to pay off the damages inflicted on Leyland Band's instruments. When all the deductions had been made, a nice sum was left over that would keep the crew of the *Nimbus* comfortable whilst they looked for another job, and the prospect of convoy work with Eddie Stormbart need not feature at this point. The captain called for a celebration.

The following day Puffy walked in on his captain, who was enjoying a cup of coffee and listening to a Leyland Band CD. Since he had paid the band a substantial sum for replacement instruments, he had started to take an interest in them, and he found their music inspirational. Puffy really didn't want to spoil the captain's day and placed the envelope marked "On Her Majesty's Service" on the coffee table before departing quickly.

"What's this then, Puffy?"

"Not the foggiest, Captain."

With that the captain opened the envelope, pulled out the letter, and read it.

Board of Inquiry

An enquiry will be held at Wythenshawe Weather Centre on December 15 at 10.00 am sharp, and Captain Cirrus Cumulus is hereby instructed to attend.

This inquiry will attempt to establish if there is any connection between the severe flooding at Wasdale Head and the refilling of Lake Windermere.

Signed: Superintendant I. N. Spite, CDM

"Bloody hell, Puffy! Get Wally Lenticular on the phone immediately!"

WASDALE AWASH

Pitter, Patter

George and Martha Fothergill were keen ramblers and spent at least a couple of weeks each year walking in the Lake District. This year they had decided to make Wasdale their headquarters and explore an area they had not previously seen. They stayed in the Wasdale Head Inn and thoroughly enjoyed it. The food was good, the beer was good, and there was no shortage in an evening of like-minded enthusiasts with whom to share stories about the day's routes and sights.

Alan Brothers and Graham Hall were both fanatical mountain climbers and spent every spare moment camping and climbing in Wales, Scotland, or the Lake District. Their passion for the outdoors made up for the long hours during the week, which they would both spend in a heavy engineering works in Bolton. They were both fit and hardy, almost always camped out, and did their own cooking no matter where they went; it was the only way of financing their obsession. They had made base camp for the week at Wasdale campsite at the north-eastern end of Wast Water in order that they would be best placed to go climbing on Scafell Pike. The campsite was quite close to the shore of Wast Water.

George was woken up in the early hours of the morning when it was still pitch black outside. He disturbed Martha from her sleep.

"Martha, Martha."

"What's up with you, George?"

"Listen to the sound of the rain, Martha—it's torrential!"

They had a second-floor room in the inn, directly under the roof, and the rain was pelting down on the tiles, making a loud pitter-patter sound.

"It is George. You might as well try and get back to sleep, and we'll see what it's like at breakfast." With that, Martha turned over and descended back into a deep slumber.

For George it was not that easy. He was a light sleeper at the best of times, and there was no way he could block out the sound of the outside monsoon. He tossed and turned for ages and eventually dropped off, but he did not know that his sleep was triggered by someone switching off the monsoon. It was exactly 5.00 am.

Pitter-patter on a tent in great force was no sleeping matter, and both Alan and Graham awoke suddenly.

"Crikey, listen to that lot coming down," said Alan.

"It's really heavy. I think we'd better be on our guard," replied Graham.

There was no fun trying to sleep in a tent when heavy rain was hitting the canvas, and no matter how the two keen climbers tried to bury themselves in their sleeping bags, there was no escape from the noise of the huge, cascading raindrops. In a relatively short time it was becoming apparent that the ground underneath them was becoming very soggy. It was time to start packing up and moving before things got worse.

Just as fast as the monsoon had started, it stopped, and on rising for breakfast George looked out of the window half expecting a pretty dismal panorama, but to his astonishment the dawn was lovely with not a cloud in sight. He couldn't believe it after the night they had had.

"What's it like, George?" asked Martha.

"The ground looks pretty damp, and it looks as if the lake shoreline has moved a bit in our direction, but otherwise it's good."

Alan and Graham had had a very different experience. They had hurriedly stowed all their gear in their rucksacks before venturing out of the tent to take it down. It would not be very enjoyable in this rain, but at the exact moment that they clawed their way out, the rain stopped. However, the early dawn brought with it the sight of a very wet and soggy campsite and a lakeside now on their doorstep. There was no point in stopping here, they thought—any more rain, and they would be afloat! Feeling cold and miserable, they packed up and moved to Wasdale National Trust Campsite, which was further away from the lakeside and not as wet and soggy as the place they had just left. After erecting the tent again, they decided to have breakfast in the Wasdale Head Inn before getting back into their sleeping bags.

The dining room in the inn was overflowing with people trying to get a breakfast and sharing the night's watery experience.

"The level of Wast Water has risen considerably during the night, and it's flooded the road that runs along its side," commented one chap.

"Are we cut off, then?" asked another.

"You can get a Land Rover through. Albert over there, he got through just a half hour ago," came the answer.

"Easthwaite Farm nearly got flooded. The water is up to the doorstep."

"It really did come down for an hour. I haven't experienced anything like it before," commented another member of the breakfast throng. It didn't stop any of them from enjoying the deliciously smelling bacon and eggs, and the night's downpour was temporarily pushed to the back of everyone's minds.

A Second Helping

The following night George was woken by the sound of the same torrential downpour at the same early morning time as the night before.

"Martha, just listen to that rain again. It's absolutely pouring down!"

"Well, you can't do anything about it, George. Come back to bed."

This time it felt a bit different. In the few inhabited places hereabouts, there was activity not normally associated with this time in the morning. While peering through the bedroom window, George could see lights on in adjacent buildings.

"There's something afoot, Martha. Everyone must be getting up."

"Whatever for?"

At this point there was a knock on the door.

"Hello?" cried George.

"It's Wilf, the landlord here! You'd better get dressed and come downstairs. We have a bit of an emergency."

"Righto, we'll be down as soon as we can."

Martha was sitting upright in bed as George turned round to face her.

"Whatever is that all about?" she asked.

"I don't know, but I think we'd better get a move on."

Fifteen minutes later the Fothergills joined the throng in the bar area, and there was a considerable amount of talking going on as everyone tried to determine what the emergency was.

The landlord, Wilf, stood on a chair and asked for shush. When silence had descended on the room, he began. "You may all be aware of the torrential rain outdoors! Unfortunately, it is raising the level of Wast Water at an alarming rate, and already the Wasdale Head access road is flooded and impassable. In other words, we are cut off."

At this point mumblings could be heard spreading around the room.

Wilf continued. "There is no reason to panic, but what I want you all to do is to quickly get your belongings together and be prepared to move. The water levels are constantly rising, and we may well have to move out to higher ground. There is no need to worry; the authorities have been informed and will provide any assistance we need."

With that, the throng evaporated to pack.

At Wasdale National Trust Campsite, Alan and Graham suffered the discomfort of a second night's interruption of sleep; the downpour played an unpleasant racket on the canvas that pretended to be their sanctuary.

"Bloody hell, not another damn deluge!" said Alan.

Graham worked his way partly out of his sleeping bag to peer out through the tent entrance that faced down Wast Water. "Crikey, Alan, the lake's creeping toward us. We'd better get out quick!"

Alan took a look, and within seconds both men were out of their sleeping bags and getting dressed.

"Just throw the essentials in the rucksacks, and let's get up to the pub."

"But what about the tent, Alan?"

"Bugger the tent—we are more important than that. We leave the tent behind. Now, get a move on!"

The two of them stepped outside the tent and into the rain, and they became aware of all the other campers doing the same and heading for the Wasdale Head Inn.

At 5.00 am the rain stopped, and dawn broke to reveal a clear blue sky. On arrival at the Wasdale Head Inn, the campers joined the band of people that had emerged to take a look at the night's wet work. It became clear that the lake level had risen considerably, and the new lakeside extended to a point just a few metres short of the inn. It was the campers that had suffered the most, their campsites now being underwater. Wasdale was for the moment cut off by road, but at least its current inhabitants would not need to make their way up the mountain tracks to avoid flooding.

A Confrontation

The phone rang, and Wally answered it. "This is Wally Lenticular speaking."

"This is Cirrus Cumulus. I want to know what happened at Windermere."

"What do you mean, what happened at Windermere?" replied Wally.

Cirrus went on. "I thought it was funny when I had to do those extra two trips to fill Windermere. Now, you tell me what happened."

Wally paused before replying. He had been caught on the hop and wasn't sure what the best course of action was. More important, he didn't know why Cirrus was so mad. "What's this all about, Cirrus?"

"Don't try and act gormless. You must know what happened."

"Now look here, I really don't know what the problem is. You filled Lake Windermere and got paid for it, didn't you?"

"That much is true, but I have been summoned to a board of inquiry at Wythenshawe Weather Centre, and I have no plans to go without finding out what happened."

Wally paused again, realising that the two loads of rain that he'd missed Windermere with may be at the root of this. Perhaps it would be best to have a meeting with Cirrus, but where? On reflection Wally thought he should have it at his place—at least he would feel more comfortable there if things got a bit heated.

Cirrus was relieved to some extent that at least he may find out what involvement Wally had in all this.

Wally's Place

Captain Cumulus and his faithful engineer, Puffy White, made their way to Wally's place on the agreed date. Wally lived on the outskirts of Cartmel, which was north-west of Grange-over-Sands in the southern part of the Lake District. It was not that easy to find but was on the road out of Cartmel heading for Newby Bridge, and they did eventually locate it—and what a place it turned out to be. The captain and Puffy never imagined that Wally would live in such a grand house standing in tree-lined grounds.

The crew of the *Nimbus* pressed the door bell elegantly situated in the wall adjacent to the oak panelled door and waited for a response.

"Welcome, Cirrus. Welcome, Puffy. Welcome to Lenticularis, the family home of the Lenticular family."

On entering the hall, Cirrus and Puffy were greeted by a collection of framed photos and paintings that portrayed Wally's ancestors. Their attention was drawn to Wally's father, who had been involved in the airship business. With great pride Wally explained how his father had worked with the great engineer Barnes Wallis as he perfected his geodetic structures at the Vickers works at Barrow. Then he went on to the construction of airships like the famous R100 and R101.

"Did your father make his fortune in engineering, Wally?"

"He didn't, Cirrus. He married a rich widow from Grange-over-Sands."

Other pictures depicted airships, but they were drawn to another which was of a very stern-looking and not very attractive lady. *My God,* thought Cirrus, *she could have been the commandant of a POW camp.*

Wally could see the interest that his guests took in the photo of his mother. "That's my late mother."

"What did she do, Wally?"

"She brought the family up."

That explains a lot about Wally, thought Cirrus as he was led into the main lounge. He was somewhat taken aback by the sheer quality of everything he could see. Clearly Wally was not short of money, because this place reeked of opulence.

His attention quickly focused on a collection of photos above an open stone fireplace. One of them was of Wally standing next to his Cloud Machine, the *Discovery*, in the hangar at Wythenshawe Weather Centre.

Another showed a Westmorland White cloud in a sunny blue sky, and a caption underneath said that this was the *Discovery* in its natural habitat. On close inspection the rest were all of documents: Wally's Cloud Machine pilot's licence, the certificate of airworthiness of the *Discovery*, the MOT certificate for it, and the insurance certificate. *What a strange set of things to put on show in your lounge,* thought Cirrus. A considerable number of models were strategically placed around the room, all of an aviation nature. The one that really caught Cirrus's eye was the model of the famous airship hangars at Cardington, with the R100 emerging from one.

"Wally, I think we need to get down to business."

The three of them sat down in very comfortable chairs that had been placed around a veneered coffee table, and Wally rang a little bell. Before any discussion could begin, a dinky young lady entered the room with a tray of tea and cakes, and she placed them around the table. Her attractiveness did not go unnoticed, but neither Puffy nor the captain passed any comment.

"Would you like me to pour, Mr Lenticular?" the lady asked.

"Yes please, Felicity," replied Wally.

As Felicity went about her pouring business, the shape and length of her legs could not be ignored, and for a few moments the purpose of the visit was put on hold.

With the tea poured, Felicity made her way out of the room most daintily, her every step carefully monitored by three sets of lustful eyes.

"Now, down to business Wally! I have been summoned to an inquiry regarding any connection between the refilling of Windermere and the severe flooding at Wasdale Head. I thought it was strange, having to do those extra refill flights. Come clean, Wally. What happened?"

Wally had already decided that honesty would be the best policy. "You know me, Cirrus. I'm not much for all this new fangled technology. I navigate the old-fashioned way. I plan my route with a chart and allow for the wind using my navigator's computer, and then I follow the route with the mark one eyeball. On the fourth and fifth night, it was so dark that I couldn't see anything with the TV camera onboard, and I had to use the soakometer, but I don't think I punched the wind details into it. I couldn't remember how. I suppose I must have been blown off course a bit."

"Well, didn't you look at your PPI?"

"I did the second time it happened, but only when I had finished raining, and it was too late then."

"Wally, you really are a plonker. When you did look at your PPI, where did it indicate your position was?"

"Over Wast Water," replied Wally.

"Well, that's it then, you must have dropped two loads on Wast Water."

"I'm sorry, Cirrus. Do you know what damage has been done?"

"I don't, but I am sure I will when I get to the inquiry."

"Do you want me to attend, Cirrus?"

"If you haven't been notified, you'd better not. I don't want to aggravate matters."

"How are you going to handle the inquiry?"

The captain mused for awhile whilst he considered the question Wally had posed. "There is no alternative but to explain what I know. I can't take all the responsibility, with three penalty points on my licence. If I get another three, I will be disqualified."

Wally looked disappointed but understood the difficult position he had placed him in.

"Wally, were you involved in the problem with the Great Cloud Parade at Hoghton Tower?" asked Puffy.

"I was, but I was exonerated from any blame, so I didn't get any penalty points. Fortunately my licence is clean."

With the meeting over, it was time to get back home, but when Felicity opened the door for them, any animosity toward Wally was pushed to one side as they enjoyed her trim figure and welcoming smile. Wally could be well satisfied with his strategy, because it had avoided any bad-tempered exchanges, which he disliked intensely.

The Inquiry

At exactly 10.00 am on December 15, Captain Cirrus Cumulus presented himself to the inquiry board at Wythenshawe Weather Centre. The centre had a room devoted to this kind of event, and it resembled a typical court chamber with a bench for the board where the judge would be seated, as well as a pulpit (referred to as the dock) for the defendant—or in this case, the person helping with inquiries. A table placed just below the bench accommodated a lady who recorded the details of the inquiry. The only difference between this place and a court was the fact that there were no lawyers or barristers for the prosecution or defence, although there was a barrister in attendance in case any legal advice was needed. The scenario was forbidding, to say the least; one could be left in no doubt about how serious matters were. To add to the anxiety of the captain, he had very fresh memories of a recent attendance that he had found most unpleasant.

The inquiry bench was composed of Mr I. N. Spite, CDM; the Superintendant of the Centre; Mr Samuel Humbug, Keswick Borough surveyor; and Miss Penny Pincher, the Lakeland councillor for Wasdale Head. Mr Spite headed the inquiry board.

The captain was escorted to the dock and invited to sit down. There was no swearing in to take place because this was not a court of law.

Proceedings began with Mr Spite. "Captain Cumulus, am I correct in saying that you were given the job of filling Lake Windermere using your Cloud Machine, the *Nimbus*?"

"That's correct, Mr Spite."

"Who gave you the job?"

"Keswick Borough Surveyor Mr Humbug."

Mr Spite turned his head towards Mr Humbug. "Mr Humbug, can you confirm that?"

"Yes, that's correct."

Mr Spite turned back to question the captain. "Tell me how you planned to do the job, Captain."

"I had calculated that it would take fifty drops to fill Lake Windermere, and if I did it on weekday nights, I could have it done in ten weeks. Three months had been allowed for the job, so that meant I would have a safety margin of two weeks."

"And what was the intensity of each rainfall?"

"The *Nimbus* had to take on the form of a Manchester Black for each mission, and for the drop to be accomplished in one hour, I had to set the dispensers to a torrential rain setting."

The inquiry board looked at each other in a knowing way and had a few mumblings between them before the captain was addressed again. "How did you acquire the rain water?"

"I got it from Loch Ness in Scotland which is composed of grade-three water, just like Windermere had been. I got clearance to use that loch."

"Did everything go according to plan?"

"Not exactly. I completed the first drop on Monday, September 28, and everything went well for the first eight weeks. In the eighth week the *Nimbus* developed a problem which took a week to sort out with Black, Black & Blackmore's, and so I had to miss a week out."

"What happened during the week you missed out?"

"I had a week off with my engineer, Mr White."

Puffy sat at the back of the room in a spectator's gallery, and he was quite flattered by his boss's reference to him as Mr White. *A rare title indeed,* he thought.

"Did you not have a contingency plan?"

"Yes, I did."

"Well, go on, Captain, tell the board what it was."

Cirrus was getting a bit hot under the collar. He had hoped to keep Wally Lenticular out of the frame, but that was not going to happen. "Mr Lenticular took over for week nine with the *Discovery*."

"Was he up to speed with the detailed plan?"

"Yes he was, Mr Spite."

Miss Pincher started to take an increased interest at this point and asked, "What are the dates of the drops Mr Lenticular performed, Mr Cumulus?"

Cirrus was never amused when people ignored his rank, which had been hard-earned, but that could not avoid him having to answer the question. "Mr Lenticular made rain on Monday night November 23 through to Friday November 27. Five drops in total."

Miss Pincher continued. "What happened after that?"

"I took over the job again."

"And did you finish in ten weeks as you planned?"

"No, I ran into the eleventh week. I had to do an extra two drops."

"So what were the total drops made to fill Lake Windermere?"

"Fifty-two."

"Did that not surprise you, Mr Cumulus?" Miss Pincher asked.

"Up to a point. Making rain is sometimes not so precise," replied the captain.

At this point the board took a break to consider the proceedings so far. Puffy joined the captain, who was looking rather glum. "How do you think it's going Captain?" Puffy inquired.

"I think it's not looking too good. They are going to get to the bottom of things."

Shortly the board resumed, and its members took their place on the bench as Cirrus re-entered the dock. Mr Spite began the proceedings again. "Captain Cumulus, we have concluded that when the *Discovery* had taken over from the *Nimbus*, two of the drops that should have taken place at Windermere took place at Wast Water instead. Would you concede that that is the most likely thing to have happened? Would you agree with the board?"

"I would agree that two drops intended for Windermere had gone astray, but where does Wast Water come into it?"

Miss Pincher was almost on her feet when she exploded with the comment, "That's where the damn rain fell and caused severe flooding in Wasdale Head! Rain, I might add, that should have poured down on Winderemere."

Mr Humbug, who had said nothing up to this point, broke his silence. "Mr Cumulus, can you tell us how efficient you believe Mr Lenticular to be?"

This put Cirrus in a difficult position. "The *Discovery* has all the latest technology onboard."

"Come come, Mr Cumulus. The question referred to the abilities of Mr Lenticular, not his Cloud Machine."

"Mr Lenticular tended to like the old methods best," replied the captain.

"And how good was he with the new methods?" pressed the Keswick Borough surveyor.

"That's difficult for me to answer."

"Your loyalty is commendable, but may I remind you that you were responsible for this job, and a hefty penalty could be incurred if the board finds you the culprit."

At this the captain capitulated. “It is true to say that Mr Lenticular was not as familiar with all the new technology on the *Discovery* as maybe he ought to be.”

Mr Humbug pressed the Captain further. “Did that lack of familiarity extend to the navigation aids?”

“Yes, I suppose it did.”

“When you realised that you had to make two extra drops on Windermere, why did you not tell me?” the surveyor asked.

“I didn’t see any point. I wasn’t aware that two drops had been missed. I simply thought that that was typical of how imprecise these things could be.”

“Did Mr Lenticular not tell you what had happened?”

“No.”

At that point the board took another break to conclude its findings.

When the board reconvened, it was Miss Pincher who opened proceedings. “The board has concluded that on the nights of November 26 and 27, Mr Lenticular, acting on your behalf, mistakenly made torrential downpours on Wast Water that caused flooding at both Wasdale Head and the southern end of the lake. The flooding caused damage to several properties and campsites, the full cost of which is still being assessed, and it is now necessary to arrange for the level of the lake to be lowered, which will involve additional expense.”

Mr Spite then took over by announcing that in view of the fact that Mr Lenticular had been part of the plan agreed by the Keswick Borough surveyor, and because Mr Lenticular had not informed the captain of what had happened, the board had decided not to award any endorsement points to his Cloud Machine operator’s licence. However, some responsibility must be borne by him for not vetting his stand-in as comprehensively as he should have done, and consequently he would receive a caution. The board had also concluded that the cost of the damage plus costs incurred by lowering the level of Wast Water would have to be borne by Mr Lenticular’s insurance.

With a great sigh of relief, the captain headed for home with his faithful engineer. He was relieved that he had not come out of the situation with anything worse than a caution, but he didn't relish breaking the news to Wally that his insurance would have to bear the cost.

A few days later, a bulletin issued by the Weather Centre in Wythenshawe arrived, and in it was the following notice.

Due to unforeseen circumstances, Wast Water in the Lake District is over-spilling.

Applications are invited from Cloud Machine owners to lower its level. All applicants must have a Cloud Machine fitted with all the latest navigation technology and must be fully conversant with its operation. Fee to be negotiated.
Applications accompanied by a detailed plan
to: Keswick Borough Surveyor
Water Street,
Keswick,
H20 C02

Don't go there, thought the captain, and he didn't.

A MISSING WINDRUSH

A Newspaper Story

Captain Cumulus was settled in his favourite chair in the living room of his Slaidburn home. The view from the window today was one of a sunshine-blessed countryside made up of rolling hills, many trees, a meandering river, and a village with a church tower. Sheep and cattle put the final touches to something that many an artist had recorded on canvas. Today Cirrus Cumulus was at peace with the world, and his recent attendance at a board of inquiry was completely forgotten. The money he had received for filling Lake Windermere had solved all of his financial concerns, and although it was not without blemish, he could consider himself as being back in the world of work. There was no reason to think about returning to his out-of-the-way place at Ballyhalbert; there was no embarrassment now to hide away from anymore, although it was perhaps best not to dwell on that subject for too long.

At the usual mid-morning time, Puffy came bouncing into the room with tea and biscuits, a paper, and the morning post.

"Here you are, Captain, your favourite cup of tea."

"Have you prepared it as I like it?"

"As always, Captain: stirred anti-clockwise at twelve miles per hour twenty times."

"Well done, Puffy."

"Here's the morning paper, and there's quite a batch of letters this morning."

The captain thanked Puffy and scanned the front page of the paper, which he always referred to as the Daily Gloom, delivered to top up one's level of depression. His eyes were drawn to a small heading.

Mid-air Collision Results in the Disappearance of an Aircraft

With his appetite whetted, the captain read on.

> At 1300 hours GMT, two aircraft collided in mid-air over the Atlantic Ocean. The aircraft had been part of a large formation heading for Algeria. Following the collision, one aircraft was seen to fall behind the formation and drift off in a north-easterly direction. All contact with the aircraft was lost, and the emergency services have been alerted. No injuries were sustained by the crew of the other aircraft involved, and it continued on its mission to Algeria. The pilot of the missing aircraft is quoted as being Miss Lucy Windrush.

Bless my soul, thought the Captain. *Lucy Windrush!* Could she be Abigail's sister, and didn't this sound like one of Eddie Stormbart's convoys? It was typical of the government not to give away the details of its weather making capacity.

"Puffy, come and join me for a moment, will you?"

I'm being asked to join the captain in the middle of his mid-morning cuppa? How unusual, thought Puffy.

"Just take a look at this newspaper story and tell me what you think," the captain said.

Puffy scanned the report and then looked at the captain with a degree of disdain. "I'll bet that's Abigail Windrush's sister. It all sounds like one of them foreign aid convoys that Eddie Stormbart is doing for the government. Lucy got a job working for Eddie."

"That's just what I thought," said the captain.

"Surely the Weather Centre would send out a bulletin regarding something like that. Is there anything in this morning's post?"

"I haven't opened it yet. Let's have a look." After rummaging through the morning's mail delivery, it didn't take long to come across two envelopes marked OHMS and stamped in Manchester. "Let me open this one first, Puffy."

The first letter contained an important bulletin from Wythenshawe Weather Centre.

Air Incident

On Wednesday, January 9, 2013, a convoy of Cloud Machines en route to Algeria with foreign aid suffered an air incident. The convoy, No. UK/RAIN/AID/10, was made up of 100 machines under contract to the Aid Provision Manager, Mr E. Stormbart. At 1300 hours the machine *Softly Blows,* captained by Miss Lucy Windrush, appeared to lose power. The machine following behind, the *Flier*, was in mid-air collision with it. All contact with the *Softly Blows* was lost, and the machine drifted off on the south-westerly wind and disappeared from view.

The collision occurred over the Atlantic Ocean west of Ireland at position 52°53' north, 14°00' west.

The captain of the *Flier* was able to establish that his machine had sustained no more than a few dents, and all systems were functioning. The convoy is continuing on to its destination.

All Cloud Machine owners operating over Northern Ireland, Scotland, and in the sea areas Rockall, Malin, Bailey, Hebrides, Faroes, and South East Iceland, are requested to keep a strong lookout for the *Softly Blows* and report any findings immediately.

Air Incident Number: 777-666-888

"Well, that confirms what we suspected," said Captain Cumulus. With that he started to open the second letter. The contents came as no surprise.

Emergency Planning Meeting

All Cloud Machine owners not contracted to Mr E. Stormbart are to attend an emergency planning meeting at Wythenshawe Weather Centre on Friday, January 11, at 9.30 am sharp. The purpose of this emergency meeting is to formulate a plan of action to locate and recover the Cloud Machine *Softly Blows* and her skipper, Lucy Windrush.

All those skippers temporarily suspended will have their suspensions lifted forthwith on provision that they fully co-operate in the search-and-rescue operation.

You will be notified if any changes to this notice become necessary.

Signed: Superintendant I. N. Spite, CDM

"Well, Puffy, looks like we have another job on our hands."

A Summary

The operations room at Wythenshawe Weather Centre was rarely used, but it was fully equipped for its role. The walls displayed all kinds of information regarding the Coast Guard, RNLI lifeboats, search and rescue helicopters, the police, hospitals, and so on. Charts covering the whole world were available in a side store, and modern technology was represented by a number of computers, one of which displayed the current weather and another which gave details of the daily tidal changes and currents as well as sea states.

Captain Cumulus and his engineer were surprised at the number of owners that had turned up for the planning meeting, but then, Lucy Windrush was an attractive and popular young colleague. Some twenty-five skippers were present, and it was good to see Wally Lenticular and Windy Blower amongst the throng. Windy, along with nearly everyone else present, had been suspended for his part in emptying Lake Windermere; most other owners were under contract to Eddie Stormbart and were away on foreign aid duties. Abigail Windrush was also present, but that was not surprising given that it was her sister who was missing. Abigail was distraught and didn't look fit to be partaking in anything, but no doubt she was anxious to see what the plan would be. One of the owners present that did surprise the captain was Albertino Insomnia, skipper of the *Astro*. Albertino was under contract to Eddie Stormbart, but after not being able to sleep for a week, he had forgotten about the contract and hence forgot to join the convoy on its journey to Algeria.

At 9.30 am sharp, the superintendant, Mr I. N. Spite, and an unfamiliar Royal Navy commander walked into the ops room. Those present rapidly took their seats, and a hush descended as they all peered in earnest at the two individuals who were about to start proceedings. It was Mr Spite who addressed the congregation first.

"Let me start by thanking you all for making yourselves available for this operation. I'm sure that Miss Abigail Windrush will be grateful for your support in attempting to locate and recover her sister Lucy. Allow me to convey to you, Miss Windrush, our sincere wishes that we may bring this situation to a happy conclusion for you."

"Get on with it, you old windbag," shouted someone from the back of the audience.

Mr Spite cleared his throat before he spoke again.

"Allow me to introduce Commander T. Chaos, RN, who will be taking charge of this operation."

The commander was an imposing figure when he got to his feet, and there was not much likelihood that he would suffer any interruptions. "Ladies and gentlemen, I want to explain to you what we think may have happened to the *Softly Blows* and her skipper."

At this point the room darkened, and on a large screen behind the commander a map appeared showing the United Kingdom, Ireland, and a large portion of the Atlantic Ocean. There was a symbol in a position over the Atlantic to the west of Ireland, and the commander pointed to it with a long stick.

"This is where the mid-air collision occurred between the *Softly Blows,* which had suddenly slowed down, and the *Flier*. We assume that the *Softly Blows* had suffered a loss of power. From that moment all contact with the *Softly Blows* was lost, and the assumption is that in the collision the *Softly Blows* transmitter and receiver antennae had been damaged." The commander then quoted the latitude and longitude of the impact position before continuing. "After the collision, the *Softly Blows* was observed drifting north-east—that is to say, in the opposite direction of the convoy. This is what we would expect if the *Softly Blows* had no power and the wind was a south-westerly. If the *Softly Blows* was being propelled by the wind, the expected track would be as shown."

A long line appeared on the map and extended from the point of impact in a north-easterly direction, passing between the islands of Barra and Tiree before crossing over the Isle of Skye. The line then continued to skirt the west side of Scotland before reaching Ullapool, and from there it continued over the mainland before reaching the North Atlantic Ocean at a point on the coast between the towns of Tongue and Thurso.

"This is the track I have predicted that the *Softly Blows* will be travelling on, and given that the wind is very light, I estimate that by noon tomorrow it should be at approximately this position." The commander pointed to a spot between the islands of Barra and Tiree. "The approximate position is 56°45' north, 07°00' west, but that might be affected by any changes in wind strength or direction. Its heading is 040°, and its air speed is about five knots. Due to the assumed loss of power on board the *Softly Blows,* it will be experiencing a loss of buoyancy that will affect its ability to maintain a constant altitude. The convoy was flying at five thousand feet, and it is my prediction that by noon tomorrow it will have descended to two thousand feet." After a slight pause the commander said, "Ladies and gentlemen, that's the summary of the situation."

There was plenty of information for everyone to digest, but like all congregations of human beings, their digestive systems had a very marked, vociferous characteristic, and the noise level ascended into a high number of decibels.

A Search Plan

Commander Chaos looked seriously in the direction of his audience. Upon recognising that he was about to say something of importance, the majority switched from talking to listening. Some resisted the temptation to comply but were helped on their way by someone shouting very loudly, "Belt up and listen!" The deluge of silence was good enough to set the scene for any theatre drama, and the commander played his part accordingly.

"This is the plan." He paused before continuing. It was a pause that had a similarity to the one at a dentist, where the patient is aware of the drill being switched on, and then there is a wait before it starts. Adrenalin was at work. "Each one of you must depart Wythenshawe Weather Centre tonight under cover of darkness and proceed due west to reach the Irish

Sea. On arrival, you must atomise the water required to give your machines cloud cover; Cumberland Greys will do. Then each one of you is to proceed to Fleetwood in time to depart from that location in convoy at exactly 0800 hours tomorrow morning."

A momentary conversation broke out, but it was soon terminated as the commander continued. "Set your altimeters by getting a QNH (sea level pressure reading) from Blackpool Airport and then ascend to five thousand feet before moving off on a heading of 324°, which will allow you to intercept the *Softly Blows* at noon. The distance is 220 nautical miles."

"But that only gives us four hours to reach her!" commented one of the throng. "We would need to proceed at fifty-five knots to cover that distance in four hours, and in our *Cloud Machine Operators Rules of Operation Manual*, we are limited to a maximum of thirty knots."

"That's a very good point, but this is where the clever bit comes in—and I must say that everything you hear me say now is absolutely top secret. You are all covered by the Official Secrets Act, and anyone found not to be complying will be severely dealt with."

That certainly generated several murmurs of anticipation, but the general inquisitiveness of the audience spelt doom for any lasting conversation.

The commander looked at the large screen, which now had the intercept route highlighted on it, and pointed to the wind farms in the Irish Sea in the vicinity of Barrow-in-Furness. "These wind farms have a function about which few people are knowledgeable. You are all aware that their major function is to generate electricity by wind power. The wind rotates the blades on each of these turbines, and by doing so electricity is produced. However, by supplying electricity to each turbine, the blades can be made to rotate, and by altering the pitch of the blades, a wind can be generated, the force of which can be determined by the speed of rotation."

The minds of those in the audience had moved into supersonic mode, and most were already anticipating the next bit of information.

"The propeller on each turbine can be rotated to provide a wind in any direction desired. You will set off from Fleetwood under your own power at twenty-five knots, and when you have passed over the first wind farm, the turbines will be set to provide you with a tail wind of thirty knots.

That means that you will be travelling at a speed of fifty-five knots and will therefore intercept the *Softly Blows* at noon."

There was great applause amongst the owners present, who seriously began to wonder how someone with a name like the commander had could devise such a clever plan.

"What happens if we don't intercept the *Softly Blows* as planned?" asked Wally.

"On reaching the intercept position, you are to fan out and turn on to the same heading as the *Softly Blows*—that is to say, 040°—and proceed as far as the Isle of Skye. If no trace of it is found, you about turn onto a reciprocal heading of 220° and continue searching until told otherwise. But I doubt if that will be necessary." The confident commander then added, "At the point of intercept, if the *Softly Blows* is not found, I want Captain Cumulus to take command. It is now 1100 hours, so check your watches and get yourselves prepared. There is not much time before you need to depart."

The audience began to leave the operations room but not before noting several details on the large screen. Superintendant Spite handed everyone a sheet with all the details of the plan on it as they left.

The commander collared Captain Cumulus as he was about to depart. "I want you to take Abigail onboard the *Nimbus* for this operation. I don't think she is in the right frame of mind to command her own machine. How do you feel about that?"

"That's no problem at all, Commander."

Puffy was very pleased at this prospect, because Abigail was not only very attractive but also wore the tightest of trousers, which highlighted her shapely backside—a feature which had attracted his gaze on a number of occasions.

The captain looked at the information given to him by the superintendant, which was headed Operation Windpower. "Well bless my soul. Operation Windpower. Whatever will they think of next?"

Operation Windpower

All the volunteer Cloud Machine owners made it their business to thoroughly check their respective machines in the hangar at Wythenshawe

Weather Centre before darkness fell. Then they departed for the Irish Sea to atomise water in order to embrace themselves in cloud, which would preserve their anonymity.

The following morning all twenty-five clouds had rendezvoused over Fleetwood by 0745 hours. Captain Cumulus contacted Blackpool Airport for a QNH and informed everyone else accordingly. "*Nimbus* to Operation Windpower participants. We have a QNH of 1,021 millibars, so punch that into your altimeters and ascend to 5,000 feet."

It was a high pressure day, the sky was a clear blue, and the only clouds visible were those currently mustered over Fleetwood, which was something of a mystery to the port's fishermen who were well versed in weather matters.

Once the clouds had ascended to five thousand feet, the captain checked his watch, and at exactly 0800 hours he gave the order to move off on a heading of 324° and at an indicated airspeed of twenty-five knots, leaving Fleetwood and its bemused fishermen behind.

"Cor, look at that lot. They're heading for Barrow. They should be heading for Arnside in this wind," commented several seasoned trawlermen who observed the strange phenomenon.

Once across Morecambe Bay, the fleet of search-and-rescue Cloud Machines experienced a sudden shove from behind as they fell under the influence of the wind generated by the various wind farms. Indicated airspeed increased to fifty-five knots, and the whole entourage was now well on its way on a wind and a prayer.

Walney Island and Barrow passed down the starboard side, followed by the Cumbria coastline, and by 0900 hours Solway Firth was on the starboard side and the Isle-of-Man was on the port. The loose formation of clouds crossed the Galloway coast, having travelled along the east side of Wigtown Bay and passed Newton Stewart as they proceeded overland to a point further north on the Scottish coast to a place called Maidens. By 1000 hours they had reached a position midway between the mainland and the Isle of Arran. Everything was going according to plan so far.

In the next sixty minutes of the flight, they crossed the Isle of Arran and Kintyre before reaching the Sound of Jura. They crossed the Isle of Jura next, and the scenery from five thousand feet was breathtaking. By 1100 hours they were just leaving Jura behind; in one hour they should reach the predicted intercept point, which began to focus one or two minds, especially Abigail's aboard the *Nimbus.* Abigail had been following the progress of the formation by viewing the TV screen on the flight deck and the PPI screen, which gave an accurate indication of their position over the ground. Hopefully in one hour's time, her anxiety would be relieved.

The last sixty minutes saw them pass the Island of Colonsay on their port side before skirting the southern tip of the Island of Mull and Iona. Then the flight passed between the islands of Tiree and Coll. It was at this point that eyes started to strain for the *Softly Blows* because they were only a couple of nautical miles from their destination, and it was not far short of noon. The *Softly Blows* should not prove difficult to pick out below them, given that it would be the only other cloud in the sky today. Captain Cumulus kept his eye on his PPI because it was this instrument which would indicate when they had reached the intended position, which the entourage did at precisely 1200 hours.

Blank and Blue

Eyes peered in every direction, but to no avail. There was no sign of the *Softly Blows,* and Abigail was getting fraught again. There was little to see in the place Abigail had hoped to find her sister Lucy. The location was blank save for the blue of the expansive sky.

Captain Cumulus acted swiftly to widen the search. "This is the *Nimbus* speaking. I want all cloud owners to alter their heading to 040°, which is the direction of the wind that would have been blowing the *Softly Blows*. Keep your present power settings for twenty-five knots. The natural wind is blowing at five knots, and as a tail wind our true airspeed will be thirty knots. We will fly on this heading for eighty minutes, and by that time we should be partway over the Isle of Skye. If the *Softly Blows* is ahead of us then, we will either catch it up or will see where it has landed on the island. It could possibly be behind us, but we can sort that out later. Finally, I want you to fan out either side of me so that we cover all of the water between Tiree and Barra. Proceed to change heading now. Puffy, I want you to communicate with Commander Chaos and convey the current situation."

"Aye aye, Captain."

All twenty-five clouds turned simultaneously onto the new heading and fanned out between the two islands, to go forward towards the Isle of Skye. They had no sooner turned onto the new heading than they drifted to port fairly rapidly.

The captain realised what was happening. "Puffy, get on to the commander and get him to switch those damn wind farms off immediately; they are blowing us to port."

"Right away, Captain."

Within a few minutes the drifting stopped, and everyone got back on the heading for Skye. At 1245 hours the captain, who had placed himself at the centre of the advancing line of clouds, noted that they were overhead Canna, and Skye was just ahead. At 1305 hours they crossed the Skye coast, and soon a decision would have to be taken as to the next course of action. If the *Softly Blows* had reached Skye at an altitude of two thousand feet, it wouldn't clear the mountains. The Cuillin Hills just ahead reached over 3,200 feet, and Lucy would have either collided with them or made a forced landing.

"Keep your eyes out, everybody—we may be looking for wreckage."

Abigail's anxiety level shot up, and she tightly gripped the handrail on the flight deck.

Fifteen minutes later Captain Cumulus reached a decision. "This is the *Nimbus* speaking. There is no sign of any wreckage, so I am going to assume that the *Softly Blows* did not reach this far and is in fact behind us. When I say go, I want all of you to about turn and retrace your flight path on a heading of 220°. We will be flying into a five-knot headwind, and with our current power settings our ground speed will be twenty knots. It will take us two hours to get back to the original intercept position. Cloud Machines, go!"

The captain turned to his engineer. "Puffy, you'd better keep the commander in the picture."

As the Cloud Machines began to retrace their route, the few folk on the sparsely populated part of Skye down below would be truly dumbfounded by what they could see, and in the pubs that night there was no doubt that their stories would more than likely be treated like a fisherman's "the one that got away",: with a degree of disbelief.

"I tell you, thar were twenty-five of 'em all in a line, and when they had passed over us, they stopped and turned round, just like a formation dancing team, and went back the way they had come."

"An' where was you when you saw 'em?"

"I was on the summit of Sgurr a'Ghreadaidh, I had me lunch on it."

"That explains it: you must have had an oxygen deprivation problem."

The conversation halted at that point to allow the serious business of drinking to continue.

On the two-hour flight back to the original intercept point, Puffy White took his mind off Abigail's shapely backside and started to think seriously about Operation Windpower. It crossed his mind that when the *Nimbus* had originally reached the predicted position of the *Softly Blows* and turned to starboard to head for Skye, the wind farm-generated wind blew them to port. Could that not have done the same to the *Softly Blows*? If it had, then the *Softly Blows* would have been blown onto the same heading they had taken from Fleetwood, and that would take it over Barra and out over the Atlantic Ocean. He decided it would be prudent to let the captain know what he was thinking.

Captain Cumulus had been engaged in deep conversation with Abigail when Puffy approached him, and he was not very pleased that he had not had the idea himself, especially in front of Abigail. It would have raised his profile, or so he thought. The centre of his attraction, however, had her mind on things other than any of his amorous intentions.

The captain made no immediate response to Puffy, but as they approached 56º45' north 07º00' west as shown on the PPI, he announced to everyone, "Since we have not located the *Softly Blows,* we are going to turn onto a heading of 324º, which is the direction of the wind created by the wind farms. I am going to assume that this wind may have blown the *Softly Blows* away, and I am going to investigate that possibility. When we have turned onto the new heading, fan out again and keep your eyes peeled. Turn onto the new heading now."

Typical, thought Puffy. *Never any recognition except when something goes wrong.* But someone aboard knew whose idea this was!

The Search Continues

On the new heading the Cloud Machines fanned out again and proceeded towards the island of Barra. It was 1520 hours when they turned onto the new search course, and they continued on it for three hours and twenty minutes, by which time they had covered eighty-two nautical miles. It was now dark, and the ground below could only be observed by switching the TV camera to its infrared mode. Although everyone had kept a sharp lookout, no one had made sight of the *Softly Blows*. The island of St Kilda was on the starboard side of the *Nimbus* at this point, and it made a splendid view on the TV screen, with Village Bay and the military camp clearly standing out.

Suddenly, Wally Lenticular in the *Discovery*, who was about to fly right over the island, burst out in excitement over the radio. "Thar she blows! I can see the *Softly Blows*."

"Where is she?" asked the captain.

"She's come down near the radar station on Mullach Sgar, on the south-eastern part of the island."

"How can you tell it's the *Softly Blows*?"

"Well, all its cloud has gone, and you can see the machine and its emergency parachutes deployed around it."

"Well spotted, Wally. Puffy, let the commander know, and get in touch with the military camp. See if you can find out what has happened to Lucy."

"Aye aye, Captain."

Captain Cumulus turned to face Abigail, and judging by the way she was looking at him, he was clearly her hero. If he played his cards right, he could be in for an interesting time.

When the military camp on St Kilda contacted the *Nimbus*, they were able to confirm that Lucy Windrush was alive and well, and Abigail became ecstatic, lavishing kisses on both the captain and his faithful engineer, who were both inclined to think Christmas had come early. The point now was what to do next.

The captain made his decision quickly. "This is Captain Cumulus speaking on board the *Nimbus*. Operation Windpower has been successful. The *Softly Blows* and her skipper have been found safe and sound. The operation is therefore concluded. Wally Lenticular will now assume command of the formation, and you will head back to Wythenshawe Weather Centre. The *Nimbus* will land on St Kilda to pick up the *Softly Blows* skipper and follow on behind. Thank you, everybody, for a splendid effort."

I know which behind I would like to follow, thought Puffy.

With that, the cloud formation did an about turn and started the long journey back to Wythenshawe.

"Puffy, get in touch with the officer in charge on the island, will you? I need to speak to him."

"Very good, sir."

"This is Flight Lieutenant Waffler here. I'm the OIC on St Kilda, and I must say, chaps, what a splendid show. Tip top and all that."

"This is Captain Cumulus on board the *Nimbus*. I need a location to land and collect Miss Windrush. Can you oblige?"

"No trouble, old boy. You can land in the same location as the *Softly Blows*. We can anchor you down and bring you down to the camp in one of our vehicles."

"That's most helpful. As soon as we have picked Miss Windrush up and made arrangements for the recovery of the *Softly Blows,* we will be on our way."

"On your way? Not likely! We don't get to see a visitor for months on end here on St Kilda, and never such dishy young ladies like Lucy Windrush. You must stop the night and have a tot or two with us. I won't take no for an answer."

Don't refuse, thought Puffy.

"Very well. We will, and thanks for the invitation."

With that the *Nimbus* carefully descended to land close to the radar station on Mullach Sgar, and the two crew members and a very excited Abigail made their way out of the *Nimbus*, through the cloud, and out into the night. They were greeted by a star-speckled view of mountain and sea and by a burly RAF corporal.

"Evening, sir," said the corporal. "I'm to take you down to the camp."

They boarded a Land Rover, and as they started the journey they could just make out the lights on the radar station. The journey down a steep and twisting, narrow road in the dark was scary, particularly at the speed the corporal was driving, but in a fairly short time they pulled up outside a building that looked like a combination of a church and a school. As they got out of the vehicle, the beauty of Village Bay was apparent, and there was a 'Welcome to the Puff Inn' sign outside the building.

When they entered the inn, Abigail's eyes met those of Lucy, and in an explosion of joy they embraced each other to the loud accompaniment of all those who had gathered to witness the reunion. Judging by the warm greetings of everyone and the expectancy on people's faces, this was going to be a night to remember.

Lucy Tells All

After much hand shaking, eating, and drinking, an opportune moment arrived, and Captain Cumulus seized it by taking the lovely Lucy to one side to find out exactly what had happened to the *Softly Blows*. He was joined by both Puffy and Abigail.

Evidently, Lucy had forgotten to refuel her machine at Wythenshawe before she set off to join the convoy to Algiers. On the long journey over the Atlantic Ocean, the fuel had run dry, and the fan duct motors that silently propelled the cloud suddenly stopped. The *Softly Blows* lost speed, and the machine behind her, the *Flier*, couldn't avoid colliding with her. That resulted in the radio antennae being damaged, and she couldn't make contact with anyone. After that she was at the mercy of the prevailing wind, which steadily but slowly blew her towards Scotland. As she reached a position between Barra and Tiree, she encountered a strong south-easterly wind that blew her out over the Atlantic again.

"That was the work of Commander Chaos—Chaos by name and chaos by nature," remarked the captain.

"What happened, then?" asked Abigail.

Lucy went on to describe how she started to panic as she got further into the Atlantic and slowly lost height. She spotted St Kilda on her starboard side, and as luck would have it the wind stopped. She rapidly got rid of her cloud by using a hand-wind generator on board to make the dispensers work, and a rapid downpour suddenly left a very naked *Softly Blows* in the sky. With the loss of buoyancy, the craft started to fall quickly, and she could only prevent a disaster by deploying the emergency parachutes and steering directly to the nearest part of the island. That was how she came to be at the radar station on Mullach Sgar.

Lucy turned to face the captain, and after giving him a grateful smile, she posed a question. "What will happen now, Cirrus?"

Cirrus didn't mind in the least that she had chosen to address him in the way she had. He found it flattering. It was duly noted by Puffy. "Well, Lucy, we will take you back on the *Nimbus* with us tomorrow, and we will get Black, Black & Blackmore's to organise the recovery of the *Softly Blows*.

"I can't come back with you, Cirrus."

"Why ever not?"

"I got such a lovely welcome when I arrived, and they get so few visitors here that I thought I would stay a while and get to know them all. You see, there are only fifteen service people stationed here, and two are females. It would be impolite not to show my gratitude."

After looking around at the fit-looking blokes in the Puff Inn, Cirrus wondered how much gratitude Lucy would be showing them.

"But there is another very special reason, Cirrus," Lucy continued.

"And what's that?"

"Did you know I have a friend who composes music?"

"No, I didn't know. Who is she?"

"Her name is Lucy Pankhurst."

"Now, that is a name I know. Isn't she the composer that is making a name for herself amongst the Brass Band fraternity?"

"I'm surprised you know them, Cirrus."

"Oh yes, I have had some dealings with Leyland Band."

"What a coincidence," Lucy replied.

She went on to tell the captain that she had been in touch with her composer friend to ask her if she would compose a new piece for the island

and call it "St Kilda's Fling". Then she'd come across to the island with Leyland Band to give a concert and play the new piece.

"What a splendid idea! But how are they going to get here, and what does the OIC think about it?"

"A supply ship calls here every two weeks from Oban, and we can get the band on it and probably the engineers from Black, Black & Blackmore's."

"You seem to have thought about everything, Lucy."

At this point Flight Lieutenant Waffler, who had been discreetly listening to the conversation, joined in. "Wizard idea, Lucy, wizard! We have enough tents to accommodate everybody, and we even have a large marquee that we could erect to hold the concert in. Damn good idea! It will be the first brass band to set foot on the island—the biggest thing to happen here since the last inhabitants left in 1930. If I get the details out to all local shipping, we can get Village Bay full up with vessels and make a real ceilidh out of it for the crews. What do you think of it, Cirrus? By the way, the name's Willy."

Willy Waffler? What a great name, thought the captain but he resisted making capital of it.

With everything agreed, the conversation and drinking carried on, with all present relishing the experience. Cirrus and his faithful engineer forgot to inform the commander, but that could wait for the bleary-eyed morning. Eventually, Cirrus called it a day and was escorted to a room which had been allocated for his use, but he was surprised that he would be sleeping in a hammock.

He slept well but woke up the following morning on the floor and with a severe hangover, which he had not experienced for many years. He rendezvoused with Puffy over a light breakfast, and upon learning that Abigail had chosen to stay behind with her sister, they boarded the service transport which took them back up the mountain to the *Nimbus.* Then they made the journey back to Wythenshawe Weather Centre.

Back in Slaidburn

Mid-morning in January in Slaidburn was always pretty cold, and this year was no exception. It was a time to sit in front of a comforting fire and keep the cold at bay on the other side of the window. At the usual time, Puffy arrived with a cup of tea, the morning paper, and the post.

"Stirred anti-clockwise at twelve miles per hour, twenty times," announced Puffy in anticipation of the captain's standard question.

"Thanks, Puffy, you're a good man."

Cirrus looked at the single letter that had arrived and noted that it was another OHMS job. He decided to read it before reading the Daily Gloom. He was both pleased and a little embarrassed by its contents.

> From: Commander T. Chaos, RN
> January 28
> To: Captain C. Cumulus
> The *Nimbus*
>
> Dear Captain Cumulus,
>
> It is my privilege to extend to you, on behalf of the Royal Navy, sincere thanks for your major contribution to Operation Windpower, which was so excellently executed and brought to a very successful conclusion. It is true to say that rescue operations like this one could not be attempted without the expertise of people like yourself, and your services are greatly valued. Your demonstration of initiative at a point in the operation when all seemed lost is worthy of commendation, and I have informed those higher up the chain of command.
>
> Yours Aye,
> Commander T. Chaos

What a great way to start a winter's morning, thought the captain. To be commended in this way could lead to the award of a CDM, but then the truth started to dawn on him: it had not been his idea—it had been Puffy's.

"Good news, Captain?" asked Puffy, detecting an air of reserved satisfaction and maybe even happiness on his skipper's face.

"Just read this, Puffy." Once the letter had been read, the captain announced, "It was your idea to move the search area, not mine, and I'm going to see that that is brought to the authorities' notice."

"Thanks, Cirrus."

"Now, don't push it too far, Puffy."

"Aye aye, Captain."

Captain Cumulus read the morning paper next and covered what he called the "Talking Club columns" (which meant "what the government was saying but not doing"), and then his attention moved to other things. On page four an interesting headline grabbed his attention.

Rescue Operation Receives Substantial Bill

On further reading, the operation was in fact Operation Windpower, and the bill was for electricity used to power the wind farms that generated the tail wind.

At twenty-five thousand pounds it was a substantial bill. *Glad I don't have to pay for it,* he thought.

A knock on the front door brought his reading to a temporary stop.

"Bless me, look who is visiting us!" remarked an excited Puffy. "Come in, come in, and let me take your coats."

Cirrus waited expectantly to see who had brought such glee to his faithful engineer. He didn't have long to wait. Through the living room door came not one but three glamorous young ladies.

"Look who's come to visit us, Captain."

"Lucy, Abigail, it's lovely to see you both—and you, too," said Cirrus.

"This is Lucy Pankhurst, the composer friend of mine," said Lucy Windrush.

With the formalities over, they all sat round the fire. Puffy joined them with fresh tea and scones whilst they chewed over recent events.

"I thought you were going to stay on St Kilda for a while, until you got Leyland Band out to perform a concert and a new piece of music?" remarked Cirrus.

Abigail replied, "That was the original idea, but after you left the weather got bad on St Kilda, and we could see how difficult it would be to sail out there in the winter. In fact, Cirrus, we have something for you to put in your diary. On July 7 we are going to have the shindig we talked about, and we want you and Puffy to attend. It's going to be very special, and invitations are going to be sent to the families that used to live on St Kilda."

"Thanks indeed, Abigail. We will both accept your invitation. But who will play?"

It was Lucy Pankhurst that responded. "Leyland Band has a busy schedule until July, so it fits in well with them. That also gives me more time to compose "St Kilda's Fling", and I think there is a good chance that we will get a pipe band to join us as well."

"It all sounds very exciting. I'm sure Puffy and I will look forward to it. By the way, how did you get back?"

Lucy Windrush replied, "The engineers from Black, Black & Blackmore's arrived by sea looking very green, but once they recovered they soon fixed the *Softly Blows.* Abigail and I jumped in and made our way back to Wythenshawe. The engineers from Salford were not so lucky—they had another dreadful passage back to Oban on the supply ship."

The captain and Puffy spent the next hour very pleasantly chatting to three delightful ladies in the nicest of surroundings, even if some of the wall-mounted pictures depicted very stern-looking ancestors of Cirrus Cumulus. Still, there was no getting away from the fact that this was one of his better days.

HOW DO I PAY THE BILL?

A Request Is Made

Captain Cumulus had just completed reading the Daily Gloom and was seriously asking himself what useful purpose it served voting for anyone in general elections. When all was said and done, candidates became members of a lucrative talking club that over the years had mismanaged the country's finances to such an extent that the money needed for many things had to be borrowed, with huge amounts of interest paid. They had got the country locked into debt. *If I ran my own affairs in that way, I would probably be bankrupt by now and homeless,* he thought. *What am I doing, giving these people a mandate to do this?*

The captain's thoughts were interrupted when his companion and faithful engineer, Puffy White, popped into the room.

"One of your favourite letters has arrived, Captain."

Across the top of the envelope, the letters OHMS appeared, and it was stamped in Manchester. The thought of an award, maybe the CDM, began to germinate in the captain's mind. He proceeded to open the envelope and was a little disappointed when he read it, because it was not the award he was hoping for. In fact the letter was a serious request for help from Wythenshawe Weather Centre.

A bill for twenty-five thousand pounds had put the centre in an awkward financial position, and it was imperative that all those associated with its activities come to its aid. After recent payouts associated with the Lake Windermere fiasco, funds were somewhat depleted.

The centre asked each Cloud Machine owner for either a donation, which would be the simplest way of sorting the problem, or a subscription to a raffle—or both. It was unlikely, however, that these tactics alone would yield £25,000. The letter had gone on to ask for ideas regarding how the remainder could possibly be raised.

The captain asked Puffy to join him, and once Puffy had read the letter, the two of them scratched their heads and tried to come up with something. Both of them had a vested interest in the well-being of Wythenshawe Weather Centre because it was the source of their livelihood.

"What do you think, Puffy? Got any ideas?"

"I'm hard pressed to think of anything sensible to suggest."

"Just a minute," said the captain. "I know what we can do. Let's offer to take a fee-paying passenger on a job. That would be a real experience for somebody."

"Brilliant, Captain! I couldn't think of anything better."

"You didn't think of anything, anyway," remarked Captain Cumulus. "Get on to the Weather Centre and let them know about it and whilst you're at it put an advert in the papers."

"Why not put one in the Cloud Machine magazine as well?" suggested Puffy.

"I don't think so. *The Monthly Downpour* only appeals to a small clientele group."

With that, Puffy left the room and got on with things.

In less than a week the crew of the *Nimbus* got another letter from Wythenshawe which outlined a number of great suggestions that had been adopted. It went on to encourage all Cloud Machine owners to participate.

One idea that really appealed to both the captain and Puffy was the one headed:

Hire a Downpour

Got a grudge? Got a score to settle? Want to get your own back?
Ever considered drenching someone or a crowd?
Why not consider hiring a downpour!
It's not illegal, and no one gets hurt, just wet.

Send in details of your requirements to Wythenshawe Weather Centre and ask for a quote.

"That looks really interesting, and if we took a fee-paying passenger along, way ho," exclaimed Cirrus, who was almost in convulsions at the thought of what might be. "How do we get a job?"

"The superintendant, Mr Spite, says ring in and he can fix it."

"Let's wait until we get some inquiries about a flight in the *Nimbus* first."

Drenching and All That

It only took a couple of days before the captain began to receive replies to the newspaper advert that Puffy had organised, and one in particular took his interest. It was a reply from a Liverpudlian named Joe Mellor. Joe was anxious to avail himself of the opportunity to fly in a Cloud Machine, and the fee of one hundred pounds was perfectly acceptable. He had no idea where he wanted to go or what to do—he simply wanted to fly in a Cloud Machine. Joe's hobby was following Liverpool FC and surviving his marriage.

"Puffy, get Mr Spite on the phone. Let's see if they have anything that might suit the bill for a flight with Mr Mellor."

"Righto, Captain," said Puffy, wondering at the same time who Mr Mellor was.

"Spite here, Wythenshawe Weather Centre superintendant. What can I do for you?"

"Hello, it's Cirrus Cumulus."

"Oh, Cumulus is it? What scrape do you want getting out of this time?"

"It's not about scrapes. I want to know what you've got in the way of jobs connected with the advert for hiring downpours?"

"We have had quite a few. Can you give me a clue about anything that might interest you? Otherwise, you'd best come and take a look here."

"I have a chap that is willing to pay for a flight in the *Nimbus* and he says that his hobby is supporting Liverpool FC."

"Blow me down, Cumulus, I have just the job. There's a big match next Saturday at Anfield, between Liverpool and Manchester United, and a Liverpool fan is willing to pay five hundred pounds to drench the United supporters. Sounds like a perfect setup to me. What do you think?"

"I'll take that. Give me the details, and I'll get onto it."

Freddie Marsden had stumped up the five hundred pounds to drench the United supporters and provided the necessary details. Match kick off was at 3.00 pm and should finish between 4.45 and 5.00. United fans would be vacating the Anfield ground via the Anfield Road exit. Liverpool fans would exit onto the Walton Beck Road. Drenching was to be left until the end of the match.

Captain Cumulus worked out a plan before getting Puffy to contact Joe Mellor with the details.

"You mean I get to fly in a Cloud Machine and watch the Liverpool v. United match at the same time? Fantastic!"

Clearly Joe was over the moon with the prospect of it all.

Saturday morning arrived, and Captain Cumulus and Puffy checked over the *Nimbus* in preparation for the flight that would earn some six hundred pounds towards the electricity bill. It was fairly quiet in the hangar at Wythenshawe Weather Centre, until Liverpool supporter Joe Mellor appeared on the scene dressed in a Liverpool shirt and scarf and carrying the supporters' obligatory six pack. His "Liverpool, Liverpool!" chant echoed in the cavernous building.

After a quick safety brief, they boarded the *Nimbus*. The fan duct motors were started and the captain taxied the machine through the open hangar doors and out onto a concrete apron before performing a vertical lift. Joe was taken aback. There was a low level layer of stratus clouds hiding the blue of the sky from view, but the *Nimbus* penetrated this at about two thousand feet and broke through its top at five thousand feet to reveal a woolly looking panorama that spread in all directions.

Joe was amazed at being uplifted into the heavens, but he was not too impressed by the prospect of having a woolly blanket to look at, and he announced his displeasure most vociferously, throwing in a few expletives for good measure. It was Puffy that placated him by introducing him to the TV screen on the flight deck, which when in its infrared mode could see through the clouds, and the PPI, which illustrated exactly where they were over the ground.

Unfortunately, Joe was still not impressed at being in a Cloud Machine and only seeing the world on a TV screen. The captain was forced to explain a few things. "I am not allowed to fly the *Nimbus* naked in daylight."

Joe's face was a picture at this point, and his vision of a naked captain did not really appeal to him. Before he could exit the machine, the captain continued. "I have to stay above the clouds until I get over the Irish Sea, and then I can atomise some of it to create a cloud that will hide the *Nimbus*."

What a funny business, thought Joe, who then asked, "What happens then?"

"Just wait and see."

The *Nimbus* made its way to a position in Liverpool Bay and atomised enough water to make a huge Manchester Black. Puffy explained what they would look like from the ground, but Joe's response was simply, "What bugger can see us above the clouds outside?"

"Just be patient, Joe."

After creating a storm-bearing Manchester black, the *Nimbus* headed back towards Liverpool, and Joe watched its progress on the PPI.

"There's the Anfield Stadium!" he shouted, and then he became a little excited as they came to a halt immediately above it.

At 2.45 pm the *Nimbus* was in place at six thousand feet, and the layer of stratus below them slowly started to head east. As the carpet of cloud moved, the city of Liverpool revealed itself to the accompaniment of Joe Mellor's ever widening eyes.

"Liverpool, Liverpool, Liverpool!" cascaded around the Cloud Machine's interior in between the consumption of the contents of the six pack.

Once the area had been vacated by the stratus, the *Nimbus* descended to two thousand feet, from which Joe would get a view of the match unsurpassed by any of his previous experiences. At 3.00 pm the two teams ran on to the pitch, and the match soon got started. The fans created a distinct match summary in an almost musical way, using a combination of chants with variations in sound level, changing tempos, encouraging urgings, celebratory crescendos, and conciliatory oohs together with the odd Mexican wave for visual effect. All this human orchestration lasted for forty-five minutes. Captain Cumulus couldn't help wonder about the sanity of humans as he witnessed some forty thousand people being whipped into a frenzy by twenty-two players kicking a bag of wind around a plot of grass! *Strange, very strange,* he thought.

After a brief break at half time, the match resumed for another forty-five-minute repeat performance that finished with a United victory. The results of the match sent Joe into a stupefied fit of depression that was not helped by his empty six pack.

The captain steered the *Nimbus* to a slightly different position that would allow him to fulfil the wishes of Freddie Marsden whilst, at the same time, descending to one thousand feet for maximum effect. The United fans started to spill out of the Anfield ground like a swarm of ants, and it was obvious from the number that were looking in the direction of the *Nimbus* that they suspected something was going to happen and then, it did.

"Let 'em have it, Puffy."

The deluge was monsoon-like, and the drops from one thousand feet had enough kinetic energy to bounce off the floor and straight up trouser legs or skirts, which was far more interesting. Within minutes the job was done, and as Puffy switched off the dispensers, it was clearly visible that no one down below had escaped. The drenching was all embracing, representing sweet revenge for the Liverpool fans. Freddie could be well pleased with the results. Joe, on the other hand, had witnessed little of this spectacle because he was slumped on the floor chanting in a slurred manner, "Shiverpool, Silverpoo, Liverpoo across the mercy."

The phone rang just as Cirrus was having his morning cup of tea. It was Mr Spite on the other end. "Well done, Cumulus, well done indeed. You earned six hundred pounds towards the bill. Good show!"

"Thanks, Mr Spite."

"How did you get on with that Mellor chap after the match?"

"Oh, he got very abusive, so we dropped him off in the middle of the United fans."

"You did? Good heavens, what did they do to him?"

"They put him on a train for Stoke-on-Trent."

"Did he get back?"

"I heard he got a divorce and joined the Stoke FC Supporters Club."

"Well, bless my soul!" and the phone went dead.

There Is No Scorn Like That of a Woman

Molly Schofield was a tall and attractive young female with a promising future. She lived with her well-to-do parents in a large, detached house in Clitheroe and had recently qualified as a teacher.

Her very first teaching post was underway, and whilst it was challenging, it was enormously satisfying. For the last three years she had been an undergraduate at Lancaster University and had divided her time between that city and her home town. For the whole of this time, there had been one man in her life, Henry Lyon. She had known Henry since her schooldays, but the relationship then had been less than platonic. Now he was most certainly the subject of her strongest desires—at least, that's what he had been until recently. Garage mechanic Henry had an eye for more than one girl, and when he dropped spanners at the end of a working day, he was often led by his own lust.

Lauren Burrows had been a friend of Molly's since early schooldays, and they saw a lot of each other until Molly started university, at which point they went their own ways. They had never really formed any fixed views about the kind of men they desired; they both still had some experience to gain, and hopefully it would be fun. Until recently Lauren and Molly had something in common, although neither of them knew it, and his name was Henry. Two-timing Henry's time had eventually come, and Molly was the loser, although it was debateable as to whether Lauren could be considered the winner. It was a double blow for Molly to find that a friend had been the other woman. It didn't help when it was announced in the local paper that Henry and Lauren were about to marry. The future did not look so promising.

While reading the *Clitheroe Times*, Molly spotted the advert placed by Puffy. (Well, actually he had placed it with an agent who distributed it to a range of local papers.) "Hire a Downpour" struck a chord with Molly, and in a moment of pique she formulated a plan and acted with speed. A call to the Wythenshawe Weather Centre established the cost of performing the task she had in mind and the terms accepted. Five hundred pounds was good value for revenge, she thought.

"Is that Cumulus?" asked Mr Spite.

"No, this is his engineer, Mr White. Shall I get him?"

"If you don't, I can't speak to him, can I?"

With that Puffy went off to find the captain, who probably would be taking his usual cup of morning tea.

"Hello, Mr Spite, Captain Cumulus here."

"Cumulus, I have another job you might be interested in, and it should be a good earner for the electric bill."

With that Mr Spite went on to describe the details, and the captain accepted the job. It had occurred to him that Molly might pay to witness her plan put into action, and a phone call resulted in another passenger for the *Nimbus*.

On a warm and sunny Saturday in late April, two families in Clitheroe were busy preparing for a wedding. At 11.00 am Lauren Burrows and Henry Lyon would make their marriage vows in front of family and friends in St Mary Magdalene C-of-E Church before making their way a short distance down Clitheroe's Church Street to a reception to be held at the White Lion Hotel.

At 11.40 am the bride and groom emerged from the church to be greeted by a sizable crowd in the church grounds and to the chiming of church bells. The matrimonial scene was being carefully followed in minute detail by Molly, staring at the flight deck TV screen on board the *Nimbus*.

The large, ominous Manchester Black hovered just south of Clitheroe, and Captain Cumulus was waiting for the instruction to move. Molly was not to be rushed; she observed everything unravelling below in the grounds of the church and was waiting for the whole wedding party to form up for a photo to record for posterity the dastardly deed. It looked as if the photographer was almost ready to record the occasion when Molly shouted, "Go for it now!"

Captain Cumulus pushed the throttles to maximum, and the *Nimbus* surged forward at an alarming rate. In no time they were almost on top of the church, and there was just enough time to switch on the dispensers and the mixing machine that Puffy had filled. The wedding party could see the Manchester Black lunging suddenly in their direction and began to scatter with great urgency, but to no avail. No one was spared from the torrential downpour of green rain, which changed the whole complexion of groom, bride, bridesmaids, and anyone else not fast enough to make good their escape.

"Switch off the dispensers fast," shouted Cirrus, "before we do any unnecessary staining."

Puffy knew what his captain meant and complied quickly.

Molly was in raptures as she saw what was happening; she only wished the scene had been recorded for a later viewing.

The *Nimbus* did not hang around, and the flight back to Wythenshawe was made post-haste. In Clitheroe it was pandemonium. The drenched wedding party made their way to the White Lion Hotel in general disorder and to considerable banter from the locals, who inquired whether the Martians had landed in Clitheroe.

There was no wiping the smile off Molly's face. There is no scorn like that of a woman thought the Captain, and his engineer had a tendency to agree.

Sand, Sun, and Other Things

Jimmy Walsh had had his eye on Jenny Dean for quite some time, but somehow he had never had the chance to tell her how he felt about her. His shyness was something of a handicap, and he was suffering from it. Jimmy was not the only character interested in Jenny. Her pleasant demeanour and good looks put her high up the desirability scale, but she was not giving away whom she was attracted to, and so far no one had gained her favour. Jimmy thought that there had to be a right time and a right place to make his feelings known, and a suitable opportunity seemed to be rearing its head.

Blackrod was not a large place, and most of the single young men and women who lived there knew each other and generally socialised together whenever an opportunity occurred. Each year a group of them would get together for a weekend in Blackpool to have some fun. Jimmy thought that this may be the chance he was looking for. If he could get Jenny to himself at some point—and that was assuming she would go—he could take advantage and seek the intimacy for which he so longed. As luck would have it, Jenny had decided to go on the trip and railway tickets and a hotel for the party had been booked.

As the weekend approached, the advanced weather forecast was consulted, and a sunshine filled weekend was in store. The group decided that as soon as they arrived, they would get on the beach near the North Pier and have a barbecue. In the evening they would move on to the Winter Gardens and enjoy a dance. Jimmy thought the barbecue would be the time to make an approach, and with luck he would consolidate his hoped-for relationship with some romantic dancing.

Jimmy worked for a printing firm in Bolton. A few days before the trip to Blackpool a big rush job came in, and he was told that he had to work. There would be no exceptions—all the workforce was required to work to meet the tight deadlines of this last-minute job that would be very lucrative for the company. This was a big disappointment for Jimmy, but it was made worse by the fact that he knew that his friend Frank also had an eye for Jenny, and Frank also saw the weekend as an opportunity to make a move. This latter point forced Jimmy into action. He had to find a way of dampening Frank's ardour. He remembered the advert he had seen in the paper, the one that he had laughed at: "**Hire a Downpour**". His level of jealousy galvanised him into calling Wythenshawe Weather Centre.

Captain Cumulus and his engineer treated their latest job much the same as any other, although it was rather a last-minute affair. This trip to Blackpool could possibly be the last job required to earn the money the Weather Centre needed to pay the electricity bill. The *Nimbus* was readied in the normal way, and as soon as it was dark, it was on its way to the Irish Sea in order to create a Manchester Black. The plan was to hover over a place called Weeton, which was east of Blackpool, and wait there until 3.00 pm, at which time the captain would fly the short distance to Blackpool at high speed, and more specifically to the beach area around North Pier, and give everyone there a really good drenching. Approaching from the east should guarantee surprise since the predicted wind was westerly, and hence the sun lovers would not be expecting anything untoward given that the sky to the west was clear. The whole affair went off in a routine manner, and as planned a large number of people out enjoying the mid-afternoon sunshine got an absolute drenching shortly after 3.00 pm, and the *Nimbus* then made its way back to Wythenshawe.

Mr Spite greeted the Nimbus on its arrival at Wythenshawe Weather Centre. The *Nimbus* had left Blackpool and hovered over the Irish Sea until darkness and then dumped the rest of its cloud onto the gas rigs just for fun before returning to the centre in its naked form, hence preserving its anonymity.

"Well done, Cumulus. You have just earned the final bit of cash we needed to pay that dratted bill. Call in to the office before you leave—there's a little reward waiting for you."

An award? I wonder if that could be a CDM! thought Cirrus.

Jimmy bumped into Frank in the Red Lion a week or so later, and the two of them had a natter.

"How did the trip to Blackpool go, Frank?" asked Jimmy.

"Had a great time! The barbecue set the scene, and we all had a good night out in the Winter Gardens. and you'll never guess—I got a date with that bird Jenny."

That was not what Jimmy had been hoping to hear.

"Did you not get any rain?"

"We never saw any rain, but I believe there was a surprise cloudburst up around North Pier."

"Isn't that where you were going to have your barbecue"?

"It was planned to, but Charlie Duckworth has an uncle with a butcher's shop down at the South Shore, so we had it there instead. His uncle did us a good deal for the burgers and stuff, and it wasn't far to walk, either."

Jimmy was not amused. He had paid five hundred pounds to hire that useless downpour, and his friend had got the bird he really fancied.

In later years Frank and Jenny got married. Jimmy's shyness proved to be a lifetime handicap, but a fishmonger's daughter called Lily snatched him in a Saint Vitus dance one night at Bolton Palais, and he never recovered. He now spent most of his time working to provide for his wife and eight children, and he usually smelled of fish.

When Cirrus Cumulus and Puffy White got back home to Slaidburn, they couldn't wait to get the carton open that had been waiting for them in Mr Spite's office. A reward was intriguing enough, but a reward from Mr Spite was even more intriguing. The contents took them both by surprise. There in the middle of the white carton lay two very shiny black puddings!

AURORA CLOUDEALIS

The Riley Academy

Tourism in the Northern Ireland resort of Portrush had grown in recent years, but many of the entrepreneurs associated with it felt that it had by no means fulfilled its true potential. There was also a feeling that the season for tourism could and needed to be extended. Tourism was a growing industry, and it was considered by some that Portrush should capitalise in whatever way possible.

Three Portrush businessmen, with a common interest and a lifelong involvement in skulduggery in one form or another, decided to get together and work out how they could mutually benefit from any increase in tourism that they could collectively achieve. Joe Riley, John Riley, and Billy O'Reilly were hotel owners in the town, and they were convinced that there was a good deal more money to be made if they could only think up some new kind of promotion for the resort. Foreign tourists had flocked to the UK in recent years, but only a small proportion had come to Portrush, and so this became a focal point for their deliberations.

They considered fishing competitions, sailing regattas, street parades, music festivals, and more as possibilities, but none of these ideas were novel in any way, not to mention that a considerable financial outlay would be required to mount any one of them. After a considerable time discussing matters but not reaching any conclusion, they became somewhat frustrated at their own lack of ability in coming up with a fortune-making plan. The three of them decided to take a coffee break, and conversation moved on to more personal matters.

"How's your interest in the universe coming along, Joe?" asked John.

"I'm enjoying it. That new telescope is brilliant. I spotted Venus last week."

"It was cloudy all last week. How did you manage to spot Venus?"

"Not the planet Venus. I'm talking about that new receptionist in the Bushmill Hotel, opposite my place. She lives in, and I can see right into her room. And brother, what a figure she has!"

Billy's ears pricked up at this point, and he couldn't help making an inquiry. "When would be a good time to come round to your place and take a look, Joe?"

"You would be wasting your time, mate. The wife caught me, and she played hell. I don't know where the telescope is—she's hidden it."

"I have a pal who is interested in that sort of stuff. He reckons that the most spectacular thing he ever saw was the Aurora Borealis," remarked John.

"Where does she hang out?" asked Billy.

"It's not a woman. It's a natural phenomenon that occurs in the skies."

"Well, what is this natural phenomenon?"

"All kinds of colours appear in the sky in the form of a pattern, but it can only be seen in certain places like Iceland and Norway. Thousands of folks go to try and get a view of it and take photos of it," replied John.

Billy looked at Joe, and it was obvious that an idea was rummaging around in the back of their minds. Joe started some serious inquiring. "When and where do all these people come from, to see this Aurora Borealis?"

"They mostly come from countries in the southern hemisphere, but especially Japan, where astronomy is very popular. I think October is the month with the greatest opportunity to see it, and of course countries like Iceland and Norway are the places to be."

It was obvious that the Aurora Borealis could not be brought to Portrush, but maybe they could make one! It was Joe that remembered seeing a document describing how Cloud Machines were being used to produce a whole range of weather effects.

"Suppose we could hire in some natural phenomenon and then advertise it around the world? Maybe we could attract the kind of enthusiasts that go to Iceland and Norway."

"That's a good idea, Joe, and if we arranged it for later in the year, like late September, we could extend the season," remarked Billy.

John interrupted at this point. "Now, don't get carried away. We don't know whether these Cloud Machines could or would do anything for us, do we?"

"Look, guys, just leave this with me. I will make some inquiries, and as soon as I know anything, I will let you know."

With the business out of the way, the conversation turned to the physical attributes of a certain receptionist with planetary connections.

Wythenshawe Considers

It was most unusual for the superintendant of Wythenshawe Weather Centre to ask the skipper of the *Nimbus* to give his advice, and hence Cirrus Cumulus made his way to Mr Spite's office greatly intrigued.

"Come in, Cirrus."

That is most unusual as well, thought the *Nimbus* skipper.

"I need your advice, Cirrus."

"What about?"

"I have had an inquiry from a certain Joe Riley from Portrush. It's difficult to picture what exactly he is after, but in essence he wants to know if we can provide a unique daytime display of weather that could be used to attract tourists."

"Has he given any clue as to what he is looking for?"

"He has mentioned the Aurora Borealis and said he wants something on a par with that."

"That's a pretty tall order. I don't know what to suggest."

A certain amount of head scratching and memory searching was called for. That started the beginning of an idea. Cirrus began. "Do you remember the Great Cloud Parade that we performed at Hoghton Tower?"

Mr Spite did not want reminding about it—it brought back painful memories—but Cirrus carried on.

"We produced some special effects in the form of thunder and lightning and angel rays."

"Yes, I remember that, but I don't think thunder and lightning is something that would go down as unique."

"What about the coloured cloud that we produced for that wedding in Clitheroe?"

"Now, that's an idea. Suppose we provided a flypast of differently coloured clouds?"

Cirrus thought this was a particularly interesting idea, and with Portrush being on the coast, the cloud flypast could be over the town's seafront. That way they could each produce a coloured angel ray (a rain stick) at different intervals. That would be pretty unique, would it not?

"Cirrus I think we've got something here. Let me get back to Joe Riley, and then we will talk again."

The Riley trio was now presenting itself as the Riley Academy, and its three principal drinking partners met to sample the local brew as an aside to considering the response they had had from Wythenshawe.

"I think the idea of a flypast by differently coloured clouds and each producing a coloured angel ray in some kind of sequence would be great," said Joe.

"Suppose we got a good brass band to play on the front and synchronise the switching of the angel rays," added John.

"Bloody brilliant idea! Let's get a really good band like Leyland. We can get them to play an appropriate piece and place the band on Ramore Head for maximum impact!"

The idea developed at a rapid speed, and the expectancy raised drinking levels to a point at which the conversation got redirected to another exciting topic, that of a certain Miss Venus, but there had been no fresh sightings. Joe's telescope was still quarantined.

"I remember seeing an airship which appeared to be glowing. It was very effective in the dark. Maybe it would have even more impact if we did the flypast at night with clouds that glow. What do you think?"

"John, you are a genius."

With that last suggestion, Joe closed the meeting—but not the bottle—with a commitment to put a firm proposal to the Weather Centre and a further commitment to try and get his telescope back.

"What do you think about this proposal from the Riley Academy, Cirrus?" asked Mr Spite.

"It looks really exciting. Providing the weather is acceptable, it shouldn't be too difficult to do. We could do a flypast with seven clouds in a red, orange, yellow, green, blue, indigo, and violet sequence, and with our luminance equipment switched on, it will look like we are glowing. Our angel rays should be most effective."

"What do you think about the idea of switching the angel rays on and off in a sequence to accompany a brass band?"

"I like that, too, but the band will need to be broadcast live on our radio so that we can hear it and have a sequence worked out so that each Cloud Machine flight engineer can operate the switch accordingly."

"Is there anything else we need to clarify, Cirrus?"

"Just the usual details: time of start, our speed over the ground, our height and flight path."

Mr Spite added that a date would need clarifying and a fee needed to be determined.

With that, Portrush's answer to the Aurora Borealis was on the verge of making history.

It's All Agreed

Back in Portrush, the management of the newly established Riley Academy worked out the details requested by the Weather Centre in Wythenshawe. The date for the flypast was set for the third week in September and would occur on five consecutive evenings, starting on a Monday. Leyland Band had been approached in order to check whether they would participate and how much their bill would be, but at this stage no final agreement had been made.

The real sticking point, as far as the academy was concerned, was the fee required for the Cloud Machines. When it was added to the cost of the band and the advertising costs, the final bill was substantial. The whole project was something of a risk because no one could predict the results. Whilst it would not be fair to expect the band to share the risk, it may be possible to negotiate a risk-sharing deal with Wythenshawe—at least, that's what the academy management team thought. As an extra incentive, the team decided to include a bonus if something extra could be included on the final flypast, as a kind of finale.

After a certain amount of deliberation, Mr Spite decided that to share in the risk would be in the interest of the centre. The rewards could be substantial, and there was the possibility that this could become an annual feature. He forwarded the subject of something extra for a finale to Cirrus Cumulus.

Portrush became a hive of activity as it prepared for an anticipated influx of tourists from around the world. It was hoped that there would be a good response to the advertisement placed in the media. From the *Tokyo Times* to the *New York Herald,* not to mention the *Wigan Observer,* people around the world became aware of a natural phenomenon never heard of before but that sounded spectacular.

Witness the World's Most Spectacular Phenomenon

Aurora Cloudealis

This rare scene of night time colour illuminates the heavens
over the coast of Portrush in Northern Ireland on five
consecutive evenings starting on Monday, September 16.
Portrush is the only place in the world that the Aurora
Cloudealis can be observed.

Don't miss an opportunity to witness the night sky
colourfully illuminated by nature.

For accommodation deals, contact the Riley Academy on
02244 567432

Several TV companies took an interest in the advert and paid large sums of money to televise the greatly anticipated event, which had taken the scientific community completely by surprise.

A huge amount of interest was generated by the many reports being made on TV and radio, rousing curiosity amongst the astronomy fraternity and others. The event was taking off in a very big way indeed, much to the satisfaction of both the Rileys and O'Reilly, who could see themselves making a lot of money.

Tourists Galore

Portrush was bursting at the seams by September 14. People had arrived from all four corners of the world to witness nature at its artistic best. Every hotel, caravan site, and camping site in the town was full, and nearby Port Stewart, Portballintrae, and Coleraine were also feeling the benefits. Restaurants and pubs did a roaring trade, and the many shops in the town made plenty of money from the great influx. The airports of Northern Ireland handled record numbers of travellers, as did the sea ferries ploughing their routes between Larne, Belfast, Liverpool, and Stranraer. No doubt the interest by the media had played a huge part in all this.

A stage had been erected on Ramore Head to accommodate Leyland Brass Band, and microphones were in place to capture the sound that would be transmitted to the Aurora Cloudealis. Many stalls were erected particularly for the sale of cameras, telescopes, and binoculars. Posters announced that the spectacle should be observable starting at approximately 8.00 pm and would appear in the east to begin with, gradually moving west before disappearing. This should happen on five consecutive evenings, weather permitting.

Special weather bulletins were put out by the Met Office on a regular basis, but that didn't prevent a multitude of telephone calls to confirm things for the many astronomy clubs that had set themselves up on the seafront. Aircraft had been warned to keep away from the area to avoid spoiling the special occasion. One thing that had been a surprise to everyone was the armada of vessels that had gathered off the coast for a free show. Joe Riley made a point of listing this as a point for discussion in the future.

Captain Cumulus and the rest of the Cloud Machine owners that were going to manufacture this wonder of nature gathered at the old airfield of Jurby on the Isle-of-Man to perform a trial run before making the flight across the Irish Sea. The captain intended to use seven Cloud Machines each evening, but for the finale on the last evening, an additional two machines would participate. Each machine had a particular colour of dye placed in its mixer to produce the colour of cloud required, and they performed several test flights north of the Point-of-Ayr to check things out. The lifeboat at Ramsey helped out by putting to sea and observing the daylight performance whilst keeping in contact with the captain on board the *Nimbus.*

Producing clouds with a colour and getting them in the right order was not a problem, and soon they progressed to the making of angel rays. The really tricky part of the operation was to get the angel rays switched on and off in synch with the CD of Leyland Band playing the appropriate piece. Several rehearsals were required to get this right, and then it was time to do the whole thing over again in the dark while trying out the luminance equipment. It went like a song, and one or two ships in the night got something they had not bargained for. That left the finale to practise before the big off.

To kill some time and to make a break from all the work associated with this project, Joe had turned his hand again to the use of a telescope, and he and Billy strategically placed themselves so that they could observe a certain room in the Bushmill's Hotel. Venus was just coming off shift and would need different attire before joining her friends for some socialising. Just as Venus began to change, Joe's wife entered his secret observatory and rapidly dispersed the two space gazers with a wonderful description of their unacceptable behaviour, which for legal reasons can't appear here.

The Day Arrives

Every vantage point around Portrush was bristling with folk waiting to see what nature was about to throw at them. Keen astronomers, ice-cream-eating youngsters, day-trippers, and media people had all descended on this Northern Ireland seaside resort to witness something never before seen.

Leyland Band had been positioned on a specially erected stage in a car park on Ramore Head, and they entertained an international audience of unbelievable numbers who thoroughly enjoyed the music they played. Every continent was represented, and the many visitors from these foreign shores had brought their national flags to fly.

Joe Riley and his colleagues from the Riley Academy had a prime position on the Head to observe the fruits of their scheme to attract tourists and make money, and they felt confident by what they could see around them.

It was dark by 7.15 pm, and the night sky was clear. By 7.45 the universe spanned the horizon, and twinkling stars decorated it. Those in the know were already identifying planets and the odd galaxy, whilst those who were not, simply waited for something to happen and ate or drank something to pass the time. A twinge of excitement ran through the crowd as someone identified a satellite travelling on its orbital path, although many searched in vain for the source of everyone else's interest without success.

"It's over there."

"Where?"

"Over there."

"I can't see it."

At 8.00 pm the loudspeakers placed around Ramore Head and other parts of Portrush spluttered out an announcement. "The Aurora Cloudealis may be seen shortly in the night sky, travelling from your right."

A sudden hush became a startlingly noticeable feature as everyone looked to their right and down the coastline toward Portballintrae. For what seemed like an eternity, nothing was visible. Then someone shouted, "There it is!" and everyone strained their eyes and started talking excitedly at the same time. When it was realised that it was only an aircraft's navigation lights in the distance, people began to laugh and then continued craning their heads again towards the east. The next "There it is!" was much louder, and the same words were being spoken by an ever increasing number of people as its presence became ever more visible. There was the most beautiful red, glowing cloud anyone had ever seen, and it sailed graciously across the night sky with a backdrop of stars, planets, galaxies, and satellites. The first coloured cloud was followed by a second one, glowing orange. Then came a yellow one, then a green, and then a blue. There were many loud oohs and aahs amongst the gathered throng. Cameras clicked—at least the non-digital ones did—and cine cameras rolled. But the wondrous scene was far from over, and joining the first five clouds came a further two, this time one coloured indigo and one coloured violet.

With all seven clouds gracefully transiting the clear night sky from east to west, glowing incandescently with colour, it was not surprising that the more knowledgeable were able to observe that they were appearing in the order of a rainbow's colours. Messages were being sent around the world by a combination of mobile phones and computers as people felt a strong desire to share what they were experiencing. Given that the features of each cloud were highlighted by the internal source of luminosity, and given that each cloud was actually a coloured Westmorland White, the beauty of the spectacle could be appreciated.

Just as the green cloud was opposite Ramore Head, Leyland Band struck up with a number titled "Over the Rainbow"', and in a miraculous manner coloured rain dropped from each cloud in a co-ordinated manner that added to the music in a truly artistic way. This was a masterful plan in action, and the crowds loved every minute of it all, clapping and cheering and almost drowning out the band. The raindrops stopped falling when the music ended, and suddenly the red cloud went out as it reached a certain position out to the west. Each cloud went out in succession upon reaching the same point, until the sky had returned to its normal self. A huge applause rang out across Portrush, and then there was a mad dash—or perhaps it could be better described as a stampede—as a large proportion of the sightseers and observers headed for the local pubs and restaurants.

Throughout the night there was much in the way of merriment and celebration, and the toast "Viva La Aurora Cloudealis" rang out many times across the town, but nowhere was it as vociferous as in the Riley Academy!

The *Nimbus* and the other six machines made their way from Portrush to the old aerodrome at Ballykelly alongside Lough Foyle. A large hangar had been constructed here in the 1960s to accommodate Shackleton maritime patrol aircraft, and now it was to be used to accommodate the Cloud Machines. This location would cut down on the transit time each evening.

On arrival, Captain Cumulus and the rest of the cloud crews were greeted with beer and sandwiches, which was much appreciated. No sooner had they started eating and drinking than a call came for Captain Cumulus.

"It's Joe Riley speaking."

"Hello, Mr Riley. Captain Cumulus here."

"I just wanted you to know, Captain, that you did a fantastic job tonight. It was a great success, and the show you put on was magnificent. Please pass on my congratulations to all that took part, and we look forward to seeing you again tomorrow night."

With that the phone went dead, and the captain got his colleagues around him to pass on the message.

News Speak

The following morning, Aurora Cloudealis was front-page news in all the national daily papers, with many accompanying photographs of varying quality. Around the world Portrush was on everyone's morning breakfast table, and the whole of Northern Ireland experienced a late rush of tourism from a combination of sightseers and the scientifically minded. The breathtaking beauty of nature's wondrous night sky was vividly described in great detail, and especially the coloured rain sticks, or angel rays, that appeared to have a musical inclination.

It was the latter point that led to a degree of scepticism from the Met office people, and it had been noted that a number of experts in the field of meteorology were trying to find accommodation in the locality, having paid scant interest up until this point in the proceedings.

Portrush Popularity Soars

On each successive evening, the crowd got bigger and bigger as people flocked to Portrush to witness the event. Even the beaches to the west and east of the town were packed with groups of excited individuals of all ages.

Captain Cumulus and his fellow skippers repeated their display on the next three evenings with great skill, and their co-ordination with Leyland Band on Ramore Head got slicker with each performance. The rapturous applause that followed the end of the Riley Academy's planned event left no doubt as to the public's appreciation, and the band in particular received considerable donations at the end of each evening.

Joe Riley and his crafty but by now probably very rich colleagues were left wondering what surprise was in store for everybody on the very last evening, and they were not disappointed. On the final evening Aurora Cloudealis provided nature's entertainment, with a little help from the band. The crowds were on the verge of stampeding to the pubs, which had become the norm after each of these events. Before the rush began, there was a sudden collective cry. "Look at the sky—they are coming back again!" People simply peered at the sky in a seaward direction for confirmation.

Two coloured clouds, a red and a green, appeared to be moving towards Portrush and then came to a halt. The two clouds moved sideways towards each other and partially overlapped. In the area of overlap appeared a new colour—yellow! Then two more coloured clouds appeared, a green and a blue, and when they came to a halt they also moved sideways toward each other and partially overlapped to create a new colour—cyan. This process was repeated a third time with red and blue clouds, which created a magenta hue. With three pairs of clouds in the sky, the climax was about to take place. Higher in the sky appeared three coloured clouds, a red, a green, and a blue. As they all partially overlapped, a most beautiful pearly white cloud shone forth, as if the gateway to heaven was on view.

The crowds gasped in awe of the scene laid out before them, and some of them knelt to make a prayer. Soon more people began to do the same, and before long the whole of Portrush and outlying areas were full of kneeling and praying individuals caught up in the infectious process, until the lights in the sky extinguished. The end was marked with the cry, "It's a miracle!" Then the stampede for the pubs and restaurants began in earnest.

Joe Riley was joined by his Riley Academy colleagues, John Riley and Billy O'Reilly, to celebrate the occasion. There was no doubt that it had been a huge success that would make them a fortune. They did have a slightly nervous feeling about the impact of the finale. They had not intended to create a miracle! There was a possibility that there could be repercussions, but they would deal with that when it happened.

The Aftermath

Once everyone had departed Portrush, the locals could get back to some normality. No one could remember an occasion like this one, and everyone had benefitted in some way. Restaurants were devoid of food, pubs had no beer left, and most gift shops were empty. A massive clear-up was underway, and there was a rush to put money in the banks. There was an air of well-being about the place, as well as the first murmurings about making the event an annual one. There was even talk about congratulating the Riley Academy in some way.

Back in Slaidburn, Captain Cumulus and his faithful engineer were sharing a Sunday morning cup of coffee and enjoying the view from their front room window. The sunshine illuminated the outside world in a splendid manner, and the green fields in particular shone with the morning dew clinging to the blades of grass.

Puffy passed the newspaper to the captain but didn't think he would be too impressed with the headline.

The Miracle of Aurora Cloudealis Is a Hoax

The report that followed went on to describe how three Portrush individuals had colluded to create the spectacle using hired Cloud Machines with special effects, and to stage the whole thing merely to make money. It was accused of being a huge con trick.

Cirrus Cumulus was none too pleased with the contents of the report, and though he felt that there may be implications of a derogatory nature, they were not his direct concern. He had been hired to do a legitimate job, and financially Portrush and its townsfolk, not to mention the whole of Northern Ireland, had benefitted. That was where he would leave it.

Several days later, another newspaper report contained two articles about the so-called Portrush hoax. The first described the view of the Stormont-based Northern Ireland Assembly.

Whilst this assembly regrets any suggestion by the Riley Academy that the Aurora Cloudealis was anything but a figment of their imagination created to make money, it must be conceded that this was a plan largely put together to enhance the fortunes of this province, along with that of the township of Portrush. Undoubtedly the plan succeeded in its prime objective, and whilst an unfortunate degree of assistance was ascribed to nature, no lasting damage has been done and hence no legal actions are felt appropriate.

That was a clear and unambiguous statement of support, and Cirrus was most pleased.

A second article in the same paper took the form of a denial by the religious authorities of any collusion with the Riley Academy in the creation of the so-called Portrush miracle. It was short and to the point.

In the entertainments section of the paper, a huge advertisement appeared that amused the captain of the *Nimbus* no end.

Visit Portrush

Witness the man-made evening spectacle
Aurora Cloudealis

This cavalcade of sparkling colour and music matches anything that nature can deliver and will leave you with a feeling that you have just experienced a miracle.

This annual event is staged by the Riley Academy
Music provided by the great Leyland Brass Band

FOREIGN AID

A Telephone Call

"Hello, Captain Cumulus speaking."

"Hello, Cirrus, its Eddie Stormbart here."

"Eddie! What can I do for you?"

"You can do a lot for me, if you have a mind to."

"What's the problem then, Eddie?"

"You know that I have a huge government contract to supply foreign aid, don't you?"

"Yes, I do."

"Well, my latest job is to supply water to a foreign legion fort in the Erg Iguidi Desert in Algeria, and I don't have enough Cloud Machines to do it."

"Can't you make several journeys until it's done?" inquired Cirrus.

"I could, but that would make the job uneconomic, and it would interfere with other jobs that I have agreed to do. One of my problems is that with all the fuel each Cloud Machine has to take on board for its fan duct motors; they can only transport half the cloud they are capable of. Put another way, they can only atomise two million gallons of water instead of four million, and even then we have to refuel en route. You do see my difficulty, Cirrus?"

"I do, but I thought you had contracted all the machines you needed already."

"That's true, but you know how it is—they are never all available when you want them. Some go unserviceable, some fail to pass their MOT test, skippers go sick, and some pack the work in. Cirrus, could you lend me a hand? I will make it worth your while."

Cirrus paused for a few moments whilst he considered Eddie's request. He had previously decided that the work Eddie did was boring, and he didn't want to do it. On the other hand, Eddie was a very influential man, and one never knew when one might need him. "Okay, Eddie, I will help you, but you will need to fill me in with all the details."

"Cirrus, you are a damn good man! Everything will be sent to you in due course. Thanks."

Joining a Convoy

The captain duly received his instructions on how and where to join the convoy, but first he had to give his faithful engineer some idea about what they would require on the domestic front.

"I think we will need to take a fair amount of food and drink on this next trip, Puffy—not to mention toilet rolls, soap and towels."

"Blimey, Captain, where are we off to?"

"We are going to Algeria."

"What are we doing there?"

"We are joining one of Eddie Stormbart's convoys, delivering water to a foreign legion fort."

"I thought you said you wouldn't be seen dead doing boring convoy work?"

"That's true, Puffy, but this is a favour. Here is a list of provisions we will need."

"That's a lot of provisions. How long do you think it's going to take?"

"I estimate it will take about four days to rendezvous with everyone over the Atlantic and to atomise the sea water, and then about another four days to reach Gibraltar."

"Gibraltar! What are we going to Gibraltar for?"

"We will refuel at Gibraltar and then push on to the Erg Iguidi Desert in the south of Algeria, which will take another four days. Then we return to Gibraltar again to refuel and then back home."

"That's about three weeks," said Puffy.

"That's right, and that's why we need so many provisions."

"On a journey like that, Captain, we can't carry our full load of water. If we did, we couldn't carry sufficient fuel for the motors."

"That's very perceptive of you, Puffy. On this trip we can only atomise half of our full capacity."

"That's two million gallons," commented Puffy. "Who's going to navigate?"

"On that score, we are lucky. While in a convoy, we follow the leader."

"When do we go, Captain?"

"Tomorrow. We need to get across to Wythenshawe, and we will check the *Nimbus* over and stock up with provisions. Then in the evening we can set off to the rendezvous position. I've got the latitude and longitude for that."

"Blimey, we are going to be busy for a few weeks!"

The crew of the *Nimbus* worked feverishly to check the machine over and to stow everything needed to sustain them for three weeks. Once the *Nimbus* was refuelled, they could take a rest before it got dark. Later in the evening, the *Nimbus* ascended into the night sky and headed west for the Irish Sea, where sufficient amounts of sea water were atomised to create their cloud of anonymity. The long journey to the Atlantic rendezvous position then got underway. The machine's soakometer came into its own for the next four long, boring days. It was not easy to navigate over miles of featureless ocean, but the soakometer, as an early form of nav-aid, took all the work out of it. Using the equipment's keyboard, the lat and long of the position one was at, and the position one was heading could be punched in, and the *Nimbus* would fly itself there.

Cirrus and Puffy took it in turns to grab some sleep in the bunk that dropped down from the side of the crew's cockpit. This was a handy arrangement that made it easy for the duty crew member to waken his colleague without leaving the Cloud Machine's flying controls. The onboard galley was a great asset, and the smell of Puffy's bacon sandwiches at mid-morning permeated the whole craft, raising one's level of hunger in the process.

Throughout the journey to the rendezvous position, there was little to see on the TV screen, nothing but ocean in all directions except for the odd ship to break the monotony. Not even another Cloud Machine was to be seen in the early part of the flight, but that did start to change on the second day. There was much in the way of natural clouds, but they were all being carried east by the prevailing westerly winds, whereas the Cloud Machines were heading west. By careful observation the first Cloud Machine was spotted amongst nature's creations flying in the opposite direction. As time went by, more were spotted, and as the *Nimbus* neared the ocean meeting place, there was almost a crowd of westerly moving machines, but it was not possible to identify them by name.

One cloud could look very much like another, and unless they talked to each other, there was no telling who they were, but it did not stop the crew of the *Nimbus* from wondering whether they were going to brush vapours with Lucy or Abigail Windrush.

Over one hundred machines converged on Eddie Stormbart's ocean meeting place, at which they point they adopted a common radio frequency that enabled Eddie to give the instruction to start atomising, which they did. When over one hundred Cloud Machines begin atomising water simultaneously, it is not surprising that the level of the ocean drops significantly, but what is surprising is when you expose, for the entire world to see, a naked American submarine that had previously been lurking just below the surface.

"Don't you guys know that we are secret?" was the loud remark from the sub's commander, overheard by the full congregation of Cloud Machines.

Only Eddie Stormbart had the authority to reply. "Sorry, Captain, but you shouldn't have been so near the surface, and I can't stop my machines atomising now."

"Damn it, you limey cloud freak, if you don't stop while I submerge to a safe depth, I'll blow you all into the stratosphere, and you'll freeze to death!"

An order came over the air to stop atomising immediately, and the process was not restarted for another thirty minutes and a potential diplomatic row was averted.

Heading for Gibraltar

Eventually all the Cloud Machines created enormous clouds around themselves, although they were only half as large as they could be—but that was due to the imposed restriction placed upon them by the amount of fuel they had to carry. Eddie Stormbart duly gave the signal to follow him as he set off for Gibraltar. Eddie led, and everyone else followed in a very long line that was five or six clouds wide. No one concerned themselves with the height or speed that they were flying at; Mr Stormbart was taking care of that. Still, Captain Cumulus thought it prudent to make a note of their heading. One never knew when one might need it.

On the whole this was a boring journey spread over four days, with nothing to see but clouds and ocean. Sleep, eat, and pilot the *Nimbus*—that was it, the total sum of tasks for four solid days. There was nothing whatsoever to stimulate Captain Cumulus, and he was going to get grumpy. It was not long into the first day, however, before the routine was broken.

"Wally Lenticular to Mr Stormbart, Wally Lenticular to Mr Stormbart," was the call that everyone could hear on their radio sets.

"Stormbart to Wally—what is it?"

"I'm going to have to go back, Mr Stormbart. I have a problem."

"What's the problem?"

"One of my fan duct motors is overheating, and I must throttle back. If I turn around, I can get back home on a tail wind with a bit of luck."

"Okay, Wally, you do that, and good luck. But remember to inform the Weather Centre at Wythenshawe."

With that Wally and the *Discovery* left the convoy and limped towards home using mainly wind power.

At 1500 hours the loud voice of the convoy leader bellowed from the radio of each craft. "Now listen in, you lot! This is the convoy commandant speaking. I know these convoys can be a strain on your concentration, so we are all going to participate in a little exercise that will help you to stay awake."

Puffy looked at his captain with a questioning expression.

"I know what you must be asking yourself, Puffy, but I have no idea what this is all about," said Cirrus.

The commandant spoke again. "When I say up, I want everybody to ascend in their machines and to continue until I say stop. When I say down, I want everybody to descend in their machines until I say stop. Now, we are going to have a practice."

The crew of the *Nimbus* stood by, as did the crews on board all the other one hundred plus craft.

The commandant's voice bellowed from the radio again. "Up!"

All the Cloud Machines ascended together, but it was no leap, more of a snail's speed.

"Stop!"

The *Nimbus* came to halt at its new altitude, as did all the others, but not necessarily at the same height or at the same time.

"Down!"

They all descended together, but clearly some were descending faster than others.

"Stop!"

They all did, and then they waited in anticipation for the next order.

"You dozy lot! Take a look at your TV screens—you are all over the place. Now, we are going to do this together and with the precision of a formation dancing team."

"Fancy that, then," said Puffy.

"I'm going to give you a QNH, and I want you to punch that into your altimeters and then get your machine settled at five thousand feet. At least then we will all be starting from a common height."

The commandant gave the QNH, and each crew punched it into their altimeters before ascending or descending, as the case may be, until they reached the destination of five thousand feet.

"I assume we are all at the same height, so that's a good start. Now, I noticed last time that some of you ascended and descended faster than others, and that's not how I want it. I want you all to ascend and descend at the same speed as me. Those of you on either side of me and immediately behind me, copy what I do. Those behind you will follow on by doing the same. Right! We'd better practise this until we get it right."

"I certainly didn't think we would be doing CPT," remarked Captain Cumulus.

"What's CPT, Captain?" asked Puffy.

"Cloud physical training."

"Oh!"

Then it all started again.

"Up!"

"Stop!"

"Down!"

"Stop!"

And so it went for some twenty minutes until in the commandant's eyes it was beginning to look better.

"We are going to do this to music, but you will only move on my command, so standby."

"This is getting bloody monotonous," said Puffy.

Music began to pour forth from the radio, but before anyone could really start to enjoy it, a stream of instructions was issued as before.

"Up, stop, down, stop."

But things did change a little, and all the skippers had to have their wits about them.

"Up, stop, down, stop, down, stop, up, stop!"

One or two captains were caught out, and once caught out there was no way of getting back in. When the end came, it was much to the relief of everyone.

At mid-morning the following day the machine adjacent to the *Nimbus* started to create a downpour. After Captain Cumulus overheard conversations on the radio, it became apparent that the machine was the *Spitting,* and its skipper was Windy Blower.

"From spitting to a downpour—what about that for a lark?" remarked Puffy.

The downpour lasted for just over thirty minutes until the *Spitting* was completely naked. Evidently, Windy had developed a fault in his dispenser equipment, and that spelt the end of his convoy run to Algeria. He was ordered to make his way back home, but he could only travel in the dark, and that would lengthen the journey time considerably.

At 1500 hours the familiar voice of Eddie Stormbart burst out over the radio waves again. "Right, you lot! It's time for a little exercise again, but today we will try something different. When I say A to M up or down, all those of you with a surname beginning with letters A to M should do exactly that. The rest of you, do the opposite. Let's try it."

There really isn't much point in describing the first few attempts at this particular exercise, because it was chaotic. The ups and downs were a real downer for the convoy commandant, but after a few stiff drinks and considerable swearing, it started to come together. It was then put to music, as per the previous session. At the end of all the ups and downs, Cirrus was feeling a little weary—and they were less than halfway to Gibraltar.

On day three of the journey, at 1030 hours and to everyone's surprise, the convoy commandant's loud voice invaded the peace and tranquillity of each machine. When all was said and done, at this time of the morning every self-respecting skipper would be indulging in a bacon butty and a cup of tea, but today that tradition was to be rudely interrupted by another session of CPT.

"Right, you lot! This morning we are going to practise everything we did over the last two days." And so they all started. "Up, stop, down, stop, down, stop, up, stop!" And then it continued. "A to M up, A to M stop, A to M down, A to M stop, A to M down, A to M stop, A to M up, A to M stop."

And so it went on for some thirty minutes. Surprisingly, at the end all the Cloud Machines had ended up at a common altitude. It had been an intricate manoeuvre to perform, everybody up together and then down together, and it had not been too bad, but the next bit was positively tricky, where half went up as the other half went down and then vice versa. The concentration level required was high, but it had gone well.

Lunch time passed, and the skipper of the *Nimbus* and his engineer were looking forward to an uneventful afternoon. It would be a good opportunity to discuss the world's problems and come up with solutions that had so far eluded the politicians. Their down-to-earth analysis was barely underway when the booming voice of Eddie Stormbart suddenly blurted out once more from the radio.

"Right, you lot! Now we are going to practise another exercise to keep you alert and on the tips of your toes."

"Blimey, what next?" groaned Puffy.

"When I say left, you move to the left. When I say stop, you stop. When I say right, you move to the right. When I say stop, you stop. Let's try that."

"Left!"

"Stop!"

"Right!"

"Stop!"

This carried on for a time, and then the sequence changed.

"Right!"

"Stop!"

"Left!"

"Stop!"

This new movement was not too difficult to master, but then came the finale: doing it to music. The process could not be described as elegant; it did not have the finesse of a ballerina. It had more in common with the slow-motion movements of a herd of elephants, but it was different.

When CPT came to an end, there were many sighs of relief, and Cirrus was certainly reconsidering what he thought about convoys. For that matter, so was Sunny Blue, the skipper of the *Flier*. An announcement over the radio took no one by surprise.

"It's Sunny Blue here, Mr Stormbart, and I'm feeling ill."

"What's up with you, Sunny?"

"It's all this up and down business and left and rights. All this motion has made me sick. I've got travel sickness. I must stop and take a rest."

"All right, Sunny. Take a rest and make your way back to Wythenshawe, but make sure you ascend first before going back. I don't want any collisions with the machines behind you."

"Thanks, Mr Stormbart."

That was the end of the convoy for Sunny and the *Flier*, but it did lead to some cynicism by the crew of the *Nimbus*.

"I bet he's got a date with that blonde bird he fancies in Wythenshawe. You know the one I mean, Captain, the one with the big—"

Before he got any further, the skipper acknowledged that he was aware of Sunny's female interests.

The last day on the voyage to Gibraltar had arrived, and most of the Cloud Machine skippers were looking forward to a day's break from the CPT sessions being imposed upon them by the convoy commandant, but there would be no relief today. At 1500 hours on the dot, that familiar booming voice sprang into action once again.

"Right, you lot! Today we are going to practise all the different movements you have learned over the past three days, and when I am satisfied, we will do it to music."

With that, the exercises began in earnest, and later they were done in E flat major. The immensely incredible thing was that the general standard of performance was pretty good.

An airliner on its way from the UK to Tenerife was holding at five thousand feet as it headed south for the Canary Island. The aircraft's captain could see the approaching bank of clouds on his starboard side. After a few moments he suspected that the clouds were moving about, but at first thought he was imagining it. The movements were relatively small—each cloud was only moving a couple of hundred feet at a time and a little slowly at that. It was only when one of the cabin crew alerted him to what the passengers claimed they could see that he took a serious interest. This was a meteorological phenomenon that he had never observed before. The clouds were going up and down together, then some up and others down at the same time. Then he could see them moving to the left and right together. This was an incredible thing to see, and the passengers on board were calling it a cloud dance. A radio message back to the UK eventually reached Wythenshawe Weather Centre.

The so-called cloud dance did not go accident free. Someone failed to follow the instructions to the letter, and when told to stop after a movement to the left, he simply carried on and collided with the adjacent machine, slightly damaging it in the process. The damaged machine turned out to be the *Hurricane*, and its skipper, Abigail Windrush, was infuriated. The convoy commandant was forced into making the decision to keep the *Hurricane* back at Gibraltar and to get engineers out from Black, Black & Blackemore's to fix it. For the moment Abigail would be stuck on the Rock until she could make her way back, and that was not what she wanted to do.

Gib at Last

Upon arrival at Gibraltar, all the Cloud Machines assembled to the east of the famous Rock. This was simply a refuelling stop, which had to be done in twenty-four hours. Almost everyone in the convoy was familiar with the process; they had done it here in Gib many times before. But to the skipper of the *Nimbus,* this was a brand-new experience. The way it worked was quite ingenious. Eddie Stormbart would call forward five clouds, which would then proceed to allocated positions above the Rock and then descend until they had landed on it. The manufactured clouds overlapped, but that was of no consequence, and as far the Gibraltarians were concerned, this was nothing special. The top of the Rock was often covered with cloud. At each allocated position, a waiting fuel bowser would top up each machine that landed, and it was all done away from any prying eyes.

It took each machine about thirty minutes to refuel, and then Eddie would call in the next batch of five.

The process of refuelling 120 Cloud Machines could be achieved in twelve to fifteen hours. The only snag to watch out for was the many apes that lived on the Rock. It could be awkward to get rid of them if they got on board one of the machines. The whole operation went without a single hitch.

The *Hurricane* was deliberately held back to the last batch for refuelling, along with the *Nimbus*, which frustrated both Abigail and Cirrus considerably. The *Hurricane* was anchored down in preparation for the engineers from Black, Black & Blackemore's to come and carry out essential repairs. The population of Gibraltar would have to put up with the Rock being cloud-covered for the next eight days, and that had not been negotiated. Abigail was determined that she was not going to miss out on the trip to the foreign legion fort in Algeria, and after having left her engineer to supervise the repairs, she left her machine and headed through the low-lying cloud to the position of the *Nimbus*. She was pretty good at using a compass and had no difficulty finding the ship. She had to sit on the shoulders of one of the bowser attendants to reach the door on the *Nimbus* and give a good knock on it.

"There's somebody knocking at the door, Skipper," remarked Puffy.

"You'd better take a look, then, but I'm blessed if I know who it could be."

Puffy opened the door outwards and looked down to see the very attractive Abigail Windrush with a heart-warming smile upon her face. "Hello, Abigail, what brings you here?"

"I want a lift to Algeria."

"You'd better come aboard and speak with the captain," said Puffy, glowing with excitement.

The automatic steps that gave the crew access to the machine were lowered, and Abigail came aboard. Puffy escorted her to the cockpit to meet the skipper. "It's Miss Windrush, Captain," said Puffy suffering from an acute adrenalin rush.

"Hello, Abigail, I didn't expect to see you."

Abigail explained what was happening to the *Hurricane* and how she didn't want to miss the flight to Algeria. "And I have brought these extra provisions with me," she said as she half-opened the bag she had brought with her to reveal some bottles of wine as well as some food. But really it was her good looks, fabulous figure, and heart-breaking smile that sealed her place on the *Nimbus*.

"No trouble at all, Abigail. Welcome aboard. What say you, Puffy?"

Puffy couldn't utter a single word. He was totally mesmerised by that shapely backside.

"I picked up a paper from home from one of those bowser guys. Would you like to read it?" offered Abigail.

"Thanks, and yes, it would be good to find out what's been happening back home."

That's not the impression he usually gives me, thought Puffy.

Cirrus scanned the headlines of the paper, and his attention was drawn by the following.

Airline Pilot and Passengers Observe Cloud Dance

There then followed a description of what everyone had seen, and it didn't take long for the penny to drop.

"This is about us."

"What is?" replied Abigail.

Cirrus passed the paper over to her. After reading the report, she shrieked with laughter. "Do you know what they called the dance?"

No, what did they call it?"

"The newspaper contacted the Met Office, who put them through to Wythenshawe Weather Centre," said Abigail, who then paused before reading out aloud from the paper. "'An official from the centre commented that this was not such an unusual phenomenon in this part of the world, and more than likely what everyone on board the aircraft had seen was what was known unofficially as the Stormbart Slow Stomp.'"

"The Stormbart Slow Stomp—what a grand title!"

Onwards to Algeria

The delivery of foreign aid got underway again once everyone had refuelled, and soon the Rock of Gibraltar was left behind, along with the *Hurricane* waiting for repair. There was an air about the *Nimbus* that had a pleasurable feeling about it. Both Cirrus and Puffy were delighted to have Abigail onboard for the journey to Algeria. They would have been delighted to have her on board for *any* journey they might make. It was a novelty to have someone else with them, and when that someone else was as attractive as Abigail, it was a great bonus. The very pleasurable thing about Abigail was the easy way she had about her. She had a very pleasant personality that lifted everyone's morale, and as a qualified skipper herself, she could be part of the duty roster, which would take some of the pressure off the regular crew.

Initially the convoy headed south west across the Gibraltar Straits to Tangier. When it reached the Moroccan City, it headed south east toward Fes. Abigail was not going to miss anything and when she was not on duty, she would stand at the side of Cirrus and view the scene on the flight deck TV screen. Whilst she stood watching, Puffy watched her, and he glazed over until he was brought back to reality by a request for information from the skipper.

There was to be no escape from the regime of CPT, which the convoy commandant insisted everyone participate in at 1500 hours on the dot. What the Moroccan and Algerian people would think about it all, assuming they could observe it, only God knew.

Over the four-day journey from Gib, the scenery gradually changed from a green and fertile landscape to one of orange-coloured sand that stretched out in all directions. They seemed to have swapped ocean waves for sand waves, and both were rather monotonous. From Fes they continued south-east over the Atlas mountain range and then onwards to the Algerian border, which they reached in one and half days after setting out.

After just over two days, the convoy reached the Algerian town of Béchar, at which point the heading was changed to due south. It was clear why water might be in great demand out here; there was none to be seen wherever anyone cared to look. But if Eddie Stormbart had anything to do with it, Algeria was going to get what was coming to it, care of his convoy.

Towards the end of the fourth day, the convoy of nearly 120 Cloud Machines, all in a long line five clouds wide, approached the Erg Iguidi Desert in the Sahara.

"Right, you lot!" bellowed out from the radio on board everyone's machine. "You need to keep the mark one eyeball wide open from now on. We are nearing the foreign legion fort at Bou Bernous Enero, which is our destination. To be precise, its position is 27°19' north, 2°59' west. Let me know if you spot it."

"Fort Bou Bernous Enero—what a flippin' name!" remarked Puffy.

"It's part of the old French colonial Algeria," remarked Abigail.

Within the next two hours the fort was spotted, but only just. The heat in this part of the world generated a considerable haze that made visibility distinctly poor. Nevertheless, the convoy commandant was happy that they had reached their destination. It was time to bring a halt to their travels. They would remain stationary until it was time to rain; in the mean time, everybody could check their dispensers and then take a little rest.

The fort at Bou Bernous Enero was in a very isolated place and was simplistic in layout. A wall around a square probably described it well enough, and why anyone would want to bring rain here proved to be a very elusive question for everyone making the convoy journey. There was no apparent vegetation or trees—or humans for that matter. There was not even a camel to be seen. As Eddie Stormbart would say, "It is not our concern to question why; we just do what we are told and rain."

On board the *Nimbus,* it was plain to see that Abigail was disappointed. She had set her heart on seeing some Legionnaires or at least some Bedouins and camels, but there was no one, just an old fort. "What a shame after making such a long journey," she said.

"I've really enjoyed the last four days," piped up Puffy, and Cirrus took a long look at him but decided it was inappropriate to say anything at this time.

It was something of a relief when a familiar expression blasted out from the radio. "Right, you lot! Let's dump some rain. We are not going to waste any time. Set your controls for a torrential downpour as soon as we set off again. We should be done in thirty minutes, but remember that you can only dispense 95 per cent. You need to retain some water vapour to preserve your anonymity for the journey back. Now, set your dispensers and be prepared for the order."

"Set the dispensers, Puffy."

"Aye aye, Captain."

Abigail was quite impressed with the crew of the *Nimbus.* She liked the way they got on with each other and how efficiently they operated. She made a mental note to get an invite to their Slaidburn home.

"Right, you lot! Here we go!" The *Nimbus* lunged forward to keep in step with all the other clouds, and the ship torrentially downpoured on the unfortunate fort. Down on the sandy ground, it must have been a very miserable thirty minutes, unless the locals celebrated the arrival of rain. Nothing could possibly avoid a drenching down there as the convoy delivered the government's package (or cloud) of aid. It was a pity they hadn't brought soap as well.

When the foreign legion had left the fort, they probably shut the gates behind them. As the convoy delivered its deluge, the fort appeared to fill up, and by the time the last Cloud Machine had left, the building looked like a large swimming pool—an oasis if ever there was one.

Eddie led the convoy on a 180-degree turn that put them back on a heading for Béchar so that the four-day journey back to Gib could get underway, much to the satisfaction of all the participants. Three weeks in the confined space of a Cloud Machine could fray the nerves, and the return to Blighty helped smooth the tension between crew members. That feeling was not shared by those on board the *Nimbus*. Abigail had certainly been a great pleasure to share the journey with, and neither Cirrus nor Puffy had a desire to stop sharing her soon. Nothing remarkable happened on the return journey to Gib, and Béchar, Fes, and Tangiers came and went, as did the daily dose of Stormbart's CPT.

For most of the convoy, Gibraltar was simply an opportunity to refuel, but in the case of the *Nimbus* it was a sad occasion because their favourite passenger disembarked to reclaim a repaired *Hurricane*—but not before engineering an invitation to Slaidburn.

With the refuelling process completed, the convoy completed the four-day journey back to the UK, which was just as well because the provisions carried by the *Nimbus* were nearly exhausted, and the crew was not much different. They looked forward to a decent night's sleep and a break from work, and on arrival at Wythenshawe Weather Centre they speedily stowed their Cloud Machine in the large hangar and got on their way home, feeling satisfied that they had made a humanitarian contribution and earned a bob or two in the process. It was another job done, and one with a slightly amorous experience that both Cirrus and Puffy had found profoundly enjoyable. To have female company had made a good impression on them, and they now shared the opinion that Stormbart's convoys were, to say the least, varied in nature as well as rain.

A TIME TO RECOUP

Thinking Things Over

After a very tiring three weeks living in the confines of the *Nimbus*, Cirrus and his faithful engineer were happy to be able to put their feet up in their shared home in Slaidburn. Since returning from the convoy job to Algeria, they had put up with considerable leg-pulling by the locals in the Hark to Bounty, which was the only watering hole in the village.

"Been practising your dance, Cirrus?" was an oft-repeated question, but it was all in good fun, and no offence was taken. Stormbart's Slow Stomp had got around and had caught folk's imagination. There were even imitations of the dance performed in order to illicit some kind of response from the crew of the *Nimbus,* but they refrained from adding any further colour to an already colourful array of local visions.

Back in the crew's home, thoughts changed to taking a pleasant rest away from everything. The convoy had taken quite a bit out of the two of them, and considering they had no finance worries, maybe they could enjoy a good rest.

"What about going back to Ballyhalbert?" inquired Puffy.

"You know, I was just thinking the same thing. It's by the sea and in the middle of some lovely countryside. I always enjoy the walks and the sea air in that area. It's so relaxing, and I love Portaferry. Yes, I think that's a brilliant idea."

"Do you want me to book some ferry tickets?"

Yes, go ahead and sort it, Puffy."

"I've just remembered—what about Abigail? We invited her here."

"That's not a problem. Invite her over to our place in Ballyhalbert, and we can show her around."

Puffy heaved a great sigh of relief because he most certainly did not want to lose the opportunity to see Abigail again. "I'll get in touch with her right away, Captain."

With all the details of the break arranged, Cirrus could get back to the serious business of reading the Daily Gloom, aided of course by a cup of coffee and one of Puffy's toasted tea cakes. Murders, muggings, and rapes abounded, along with pages of reports on football matches largely played in almost empty grounds, judging by the attendance figures quoted. That always confounded him—how could they justify such a large coverage? Also tucked into the various pages were the constant references to the general plight of the country and the usual allocation of blame that was now accepted tradition by those individuals called politicians.

The constant erosion of freedoms to do certain things had been a feature of life ever since the country became an integral part of the European Parliament, and the operation of Cloud Machines had suffered its fair share of restrictions over the years. An article extolling the virtues of another EU rule drew the attention of Cirrus.

"Puffy, Puffy!" shouted the captain.

"What's up?"

"You will never believe what the EU has just passed."

"Go on."

"They are restricting the total amount of water that any Cloud Machine can atomise per month to two million gallons."

"Blimey, that's going to restrict the amount of work we can do. Why have they done that?"

"They say it's to help preserve the natural state of the sea and the land. They say too much salt is getting in the soil."

"Well, I haven't noticed. We are going to become like the fishing industry: we'll only be able to turn out a few times each month," replied Puffy.

The captain dropped the paper and left the room in an angry mood, but not before blowing a loud raspberry and telling Puffy to send it to the government and tell them what to do with it.

I wish the captain would stop reading the morning paper, thought Puffy.

Ballyhalbert and Tranquillity

The ferry across the Irish Sea to Belfast was uneventful, although passing the Isle-of-Man brought back memories of the Great Cloud Parade, some good and some not so good. In fact the last time they had made this journey was in very different circumstances; it had been more of an escape than a sojourn.

After having docked in Belfast, the *Nimbus* crew drove to Newtownards before following the road alongside the eastern shore of Strangford Lough to Kircubbin, from which it was only a short journey across the Ards peninsula to Ballyhalbert on the shores of the Irish Sea. Cirrus always felt it was rather special to live in a house that was built on the site of an old wartime airfield. Indeed, while looking out from the bedroom windows at the front of the house, he was staring down the old perimeter track that connected the ends of the old runways; to the right the old control tower stood guarding wartime memories. It didn't take much imagining to see the sailors stationed here when it was known as HMS Corncrake, and several were buried in local churchyards.

Models of aircraft that had served at Ballyhalbert, such as the Spitfire, Lysander, and Defiant, adorned the house, each one constructed by Cirrus, who had become very nostalgic about the place. The Royal Navy was represented by a Seafire, Hellcat, and Barracuda. He had established an extensive library on all things aeronautical. In addition to reading and modelling, Cirrus had a fine collection of brass band CDs, and it was most unusual for a day to pass without at least one being played.

Puffy, on the other hand didn't share the passions of his Captain, at least not to the same extent. Puffy was more of a practical man and tended to pass his time tinkering about the house and on the car, and he did some gardening for good measure. The two of them did share a passion for a bit of walking and sightseeing. They also liked to get out and have a meal occasionally. However, their favourite pastime was to sit and discuss the country's well-being. This was invariably an end-of-the-day activity and usually involved a degree of lubrication. The captain was well-known for his early evening "feet under the table" stance for the start of a good but not necessarily well-informed debate, and as the evening drew on, his feet would be gradually followed by the rest of his body.

It was invigorating to take a morning walk down to the seashore and to enjoy the bracing air. In a fast-changing world that many people found difficult to keep up with, it was reassuring to see that everything was the same here. A degree of permanence provided a sense of belonging, and that was a pleasure both Cirrus and Puffy enjoyed, not to mention the friendly "good mornings" of the village inhabitants.

On the way back, they would take the opportunity to call in to the village shop and purchase a paper in addition to provisions. Whilst Cirrus was conditioned to his daily dose of the Daily Gloom, Puffy was less than enthusiastic, because he knew that if his captain read something to his distaste—which was something that was happening more frequently these days—then Puffy would be on the end of his bad temper.

Portrush Calls

The phone rang, and a familiar voice at the other end had a request. "Hello, is that you, Cirrus?"

Cirrus could tell immediately that this was Joe Riley from Portrush. "Hello, Joe. Yes, this is Cirrus. What can I do for you, and how did you know I would be here?"

"It's a small world, Cirrus. You can find anything out on the grapevine. Anyway, the Riley Academy wants to pay you a visit whilst you are here."

I wonder what that can be about? thought the captain. "That's fine, Joe. When do you want to come?"

"Oh, in a couple of days, I think. I will confirm later, but I'm going to bring John with me."

"What about Billy? Is he coming?"

"Billy is no longer with us. I'll tell you about it when we get to your place. By the way, Cirrus, it would be great to have a drink with you. Could I prevail on you and ask if we could stop for the night?"

"No trouble at all. It will be good to catch up and have a dram and a good chin wag."

"Thanks, Cirrus. I'll give you another call in a couple of days."

The captain hung up. "Puffy, you'd better sort out a couple of rooms. Joe and John Riley are coming to spend a night with us in a couple of days."

"Aye aye, Skipper, but what about Billy?"

"Billy is no longer with the Riley Academy."

"That's interesting," replied Puffy.

Yes, it certainly is, thought Cirrus.

A couple of days later, Joe and John arrived in a rather posh-looking car. They had obviously come a long way in the world since the Aurora Cloudealis. A conversation started that was to last a considerable time and was only interrupted to eat or drink—and it was interrupted more times to drink than to eat. Most of the conversation surrounded the great success of the Aurora Cloudealis and the complications it had thrown up, but they had all been overcome, and now it had the official blessing not only of the Northern Ireland Assembly but also of the Northern Ireland Tourist Office. Plans were well afoot for next year's event, and there was a lot of money at stake. The Riley Academy had been put on a firm footing after the Portrush miracle, although that was not a term used publicly. Joe had managed to pay off his mortgage and buy a new car.

Things were definitely on the up. The conversation then turned to what the *Nimbus* had been involved in since the Portrush job, and the captain spent much time describing the convoy to Algeria in great detail. Both Joe and John seemed to have a strong interest in the cloud dance, and they looked at each other in earnest as it was described.

John said, "Cirrus, you and that Cloud Machine of yours seem to experience a wide variety of interesting work."

"Yes, that's true," replied Cirrus.

After a short break in the conversation to take a bite of something, Cirrus posed the question that had been burning on his lips all evening. "Why did Billy leave the academy, Joe?"

After a somewhat pregnant pause, Joe replied. "That was a very sad affair, and I don't really know where to start. Billy always came round to my place on a regular basis. He was—is—a great friend of the family. The trouble was, he kept sending me on a wild goose chase to find something, and whilst I was doing that, he would sneak off to that room that overlooks the Bushmill Hotel. He had a pair of binoculars that he had bought, and he hid them in the room. He kept going up there to spy on the girl that worked there."

"You mean Venus?"

"That's the one. Anyway, he took a digital camera with him and, using the zoom, kept taking photos of her as she got changed."

"You mean in her scanty underwear?"

"That's right, but that was his undoing. She spotted him and reported him to the hotel manager."

"Blimey, what happened then?"

"Well, the manager tackled Billy and wanted to see the photos, and when he did, he thought they were good and bought them off Billy for one hundred pounds. Then he told Billy not to do it anymore."

"Is that it, then?"

"No. Billy, the fool that he is, tried doing it again, but this time Venus spotted him again and called the police herself."

"And then . . . ?"

"He was prosecuted and left Portrush to avoid any repercussions from the girl's family. He resigned from the Riley Academy to save any embarrassment."

"Where is he now?"

"He left the area, and I have no idea where he is. He doesn't contact me anymore, and the funny thing is that the girl—well, actually, she's not so much a girl as a young woman—is gone as well."

The four men continued to talk and drink until late in the evening, and eventually they staggered to their beds to sink into a coma-like sleep that would render them useless until mid-morning the following day. When it came time to bid Joe and John good-bye, Cirrus and Puffy were both somewhat relieved. They were both in need of an alcohol-free period, and a few mundane days would not go amiss.

A few days later, the crew of the *Nimbus* were driving slowly through the fishing port of Portavogie when Puffy spotted someone he thought he recognised. He slowly brought the car to a halt.

"Puffy, why have you stopped?" the captain asked.

"Captain, I have a feeling you will recognise someone who will walk past us in a few moments, but be discreet."

With that, Cirrus waited until a couple walked past them arm in arm.

"Well, I'll be damned. That's Billy O'Reilly from Portrush! But I don't know who the good-looking young woman is."

"That's Venus," remarked Puffy.

"How do you know that?" asked the captain.

"I've seen her photos!"

A Surprise in the Night

A knock on the door in the late evening came as a bit of a surprise.

"You get it, Puffy, will you?"

It's always the same, thought Puffy. *I always get the servant's jobs.* "Bless me, it's Wally Lenticular!" he said when he opened the door.

"Hello, Puffy. I'll bet this is a surprise for you," said Wally.

"It certainly is, but do come in. The captain's through there in the lounge."

"Hello, Wally, what are you doing here?" Cirrus said.

"Well, I was raining in the area, so I thought I would call in and see you. Sorry it's so late, but I've only just finished."

"Would you like to stay the night?"

"That's very kind of you, Cirrus. Yes, I wouldn't mind—it would be better than staying on board the *Discovery.* But I'd better give my engineer a ring."

"I'll sort a room out," said Puffy before the captain could ask him.

"Where have you parked the *Discovery*?" asked Cirrus.

"I put it down for the night on the end of the old runway and walked over to your place. I've left my engineer in charge," Wally said. Cirrus peered through the front window of his house, and there was a fairly large cloud that sat on the deck, obscuring the night view out to the west. "It may be a bit of a surprise for the locals, but I can be away early in the morning, and no one should be any worse for wear."

A very pleasant evening passed swapping yarns of life on the wind and sky, but the topic of insurance and the payout by Wally's company for the flooding in Wasdale featured strongly.

"I lost my no-claims bonus for that, and my premium jumped up an awful lot, too."

"I'm sorry to hear about that, Wally, but it was not my doing."

"I know that, Cirrus. It's just one of those things. Anyway, I'm back to earning again now."

"How did you go on after you left the Algeria convoy?"

"Interesting that you should ask. It was a very slow journey home. I shut the fan duct motors down and came back on the wind. It was just about the most boring journey I have ever made. As soon as I did get back, I got the Black, Black & Blackemore's engineers out to fix it."

"What was the problem?"

"They found a seagull had been ingested in one of the fan duct motors, and it had jammed in the blades, making it very difficult for them to rotate. That's what caused the overheating."

"Well, at least you're sorted out now," remarked Puffy.

The subject then turned to the new EU rule limiting the amount of seawater each Cloud Machine could atomise each month.

"That's going to put a lot of Cloud Machines in mothballs," remarked Wally.

"But how are the authorities going to police it?" asked Cirrus.

"They are talking about putting a kind of tachograph on board each machine to monitor the amount of water atomised and when. The tachos will be periodically inspected."

"I suppose anybody found infringing the rules will be fined," remarked Puffy.

"As far as I know, they will confiscate your machine if you get caught," replied Wally.

"That's a bit steep!"

Having exhausted the subject of EU rules, Wally made a tentative attempt to talk about the adventure on board the *Nimbus* with Abigail Windrush, but Cirrus neatly skirted around the subject by announcing that he'd better get some sleep.

The sleeping inhabitants of the Cumulus home in Ballyhalbert were woken early the following morning by a phone call for Wally. It was his engineer on board the *Discovery* to tell him he'd better get back on board sharpish. The *Discovery* had been discovered by an inquisitive group of youngsters who had thought it would be a great adventure to try and walk inside a real cloud. They had had the shock of their young lives when they bumped into the *Discovery*.

"What is it?" one asked.

"It's a spaceship."

"The Martians have landed!"

They then attempted to break things off the fuselage as a souvenir, and when that failed they made a nuisance of themselves by knocking on it and asking the Martians to come out and say hello, or they would be blown up—although how, had not been fully worked out.

"Cirrus, I'd better get across to the *Discovery* before anything goes wrong." And with that Wally left to walk in the direction of his Cloud Machine.

Wally was last seen by the crew of the *Nimbus* entering his own cloud, and not long afterwards a half dozen screaming youngsters emerged out of it, running as fast as their legs could take them. It was not long after that that the cloud, which had spent the night on Ballyhalbert's old airfield, started to slowly ascend until it reached a few thousand feet, at which point it headed out east to the Irish Sea.

In the village shop that morning, stories about Martians and spaceships were rife, but most folk took it all with a pinch of salt. It was a stroke of luck that no one had witnessed the coming and going at the Cumulus home, and no embarrassing questions were asked, although both Puffy and Cirrus were well aware that they were surrounded by folks that knew an infinite amount about the mysterious "little people" and may well know a lot more than they were letting on.

A Touch of Feminism

Abigail was coming over on Tuesday. She was fitting in a few days visit in between jobs, and her engineer would take the opportunity to visit family in Comber. Cirrus and Puffy would pick Abigail up at Newtownards Airfield after dark.

Abigail had got herself one of those nice jobs that cropped up every now and again. A photography club in Belfast had hired her machine to produce a rainbow over Scrabbo Tower, which they would endeavour to capture and reproduce for a competition; the session would be held during the afternoon. Abigail carefully navigated the *Hurricane* to a position slightly to the west of the tower and at a height that would yield the best result, although she was in radio contact with the club's secretary, and any alterations to her position could be relayed to her. Light rain was all that would be needed for the sun's rays to produce a pronounced rainbow today, and if they got it right, the arch of the bow would place Scrabbo Tower directly in its centre.

The session had gone according to plan, and Abigail then waited at a safe height until it had gone dark, at which point she took her cloud over Strangford Lough and dispensed with what was left of it. The naked *Hurricane* then made a short journey to the airfield and landed at an isolated spot outside a hangar that would be its home for the next few days. The airfield was in darkness because it had no runway lighting system, and hence its arrival went unnoticed.

As Cirrus and Puffy arrived in their car to collect her, Puffy remarked, "She's got legs." They had never seen Abigail in a dress but were glad that they now had. Abigail's legs were momentarily the focus of their attention, but her joyous face soon changed that.

The next few days were exceedingly pleasant. Abigail was a treasure to be with, and the time passed quickly as they took her to see various places on both the Ards peninsula and the rest of County Down. They got as far as Dundrum and Newcastle, but the beauty of the Mourne Mountains would have to wait for another time. They had a few meals out, and wherever they went Abigail was sure to attract attention. Cirrus and Puffy were both mature enough to know that an amicable relationship was all that they would ever have with this beautiful woman, but their esteem was raised to a new level by being seen in her company.

Towards the end of her of stay in Ballyhalbert, Abigail announced that she had a date, and that took her hosts by surprise, but they disguised their disappointment. They did wonder how she had managed to set up a date considering she had been in their company for the majority of the time. Apart from when she walked to the village shop, there had never really been a chance for her to meet anyone. Perhaps she had arranged this before she came, and that was the real purpose of her visit. A little cynicism was, however, a characteristic of a little jealousy that identified their own desires that they had to quell.

The night for Abigail's date arrived, and she looked ravishing as she stepped through the front door. The mood inside became a little sombre as each man wrestled with his thoughts and another wrestled with Abigail, which was a much nicer prospect.

The following morning at breakfast, the mood was somewhat lighter. The three of them sat around the table in the kitchen. Puffy broke the ice. "Did you have a good night out, Abigail?" he asked, half hoping that she would say no.

"Yes, I quite enjoyed it," she answered, not giving anything away.

It was Cirrus's turn next. "Was it anybody we know?"

"I don't think so. His name is Billy O'Reilly."

There was a crash of pottery as Puffy dropped his cup of tea all over the floor, and the conversation came to an abrupt end.

The following evening, Cirrus and Puffy drove Abigail to Newtownards Airfield to board the *Hurricane* with her engineer. It didn't take long for her to taxi the machine out onto the unlit tarmac and then ascend into the black abyss of the night sky before making her way back to Wythenshawe. That left her two former companions feeling a little empty, and as they drove back to Ballyhalbert via Kircubbin, they both agreed that maybe the time had arrived to get back to Slaidburn and back to work.

SILLOTH REVISITED

It's Not Cricket

Yorkshire were on top with their match against Surrey. By the end of the day, they should have beaten a good county side. Unfortunately, bad weather intervened, and the match ended in a draw. This was not the first time this had happened when Surrey were on the verge of losing—it had also happened when they were losing against Gloucester, Kent, and Sussex. On each occasion a sudden and unexpected downpour had occurred. A number of keen cricket fans amongst the Wythenshawe Weather Centre crews had started to ask questions. Was this a case of match fixing?

Middlesex were well ahead in their match against Surrey, and it would not take the remaining full day to bowl out Surrey's last player—at least, that's what they thought. A huge crowd attended the final day of the match, and the Middlesex supporters fully expected that by the end of the day they would be celebrating a well-earned victory. It was a fine day for cricket with only a few scattered clouds in the sky. No one really took much interest in the single large Cumberland Grey that was loitering within a short distance of the cricket ground whilst all the others seemed to be moving graciously across the sky from west to east. The match was reaching its final stages when, without any announcement, the big Cumberland Grey quickly and silently moved into a strategic position and rained in grand style. In a flash of white outfits, the players dashed for cover, never to be seen again for what was left of the match time.

With another match abandoned and another ground almost submerged in water, there were many irate cricket fans. By now they were beginning to wonder if it was more than coincidence that every time Surrey was on the verge of losing, the match had to be ended due to bad weather. Many took a good look at the heavens, but by now what was left of the culprit was not only a shadow of its former self but had also drifted off to new pastures. The problem for the fans was that although they now had suspicions, they could not see how anyone could fix the weather in such a timely fashion—or any other way, for that matter.

However, at Wythenshawe it was a different matter. People expressed concern that they had a rogue cloud amongst them that was applying itself to match fixing. The big question was who.

Cloud Machine owners were generally held in high esteem, and Wythenshawe had a good reputation. They carried out some important work and some not so important tasks. Ceremonial and pageantry had only recently been added to the range of services they offered, which was really quite wide-ranging. Search and rescue and display work brought in a good income along with foreign aid, and the Guild of Cloud Owners could do without any adverse publicity. True, some risqué jobs had been done from time to time, but nothing that was intended to influence the outcome of a sporting occasion. Even the job associated with football was for a good cause and did not influence the match result. As for the wedding job . . . well, the less, said the better.

Even the newspapers were beginning to ask some searching questions, and the MCC had been approached for their opinion. The current president of the MCC was also the chairman of the Surrey County club, and he dismissed the speculation outright, but others were not so dismissive.

Giving Assistance

The pressure exerted by the press together with several of the county cricket clubs led to the police making some inquiries into possible match fixing. It did help that a certain Chief Constable, who must remain unnamed, had a strong connection with one of the clubs that was in a strong position to top the league at the end of the current season.

A telephone call to the home of Cirrus in Slaidburn was the precursor to the meeting at Wythenshawe Weather Centre, at which the Superintendant, Mr I. N. Spite, CDM, introduced Cirrus to a representative of Greater Manchester Police.

"Evidently, Captain Cumulus, the Greater Manchester Police would like your assistance."

This was not the usual way that Mr Spite referred to the captain, but he was most pleased; it put him on a good footing from the outset.

The GMP representative then started to outline what the police had in mind. "We have a strong suspicion that in the world of county cricket, there is some match fixing going on, and we suspect that one of your Cloud Machine colleagues is involved. We need to find him, and we need your assistance."

"It could be a her," the captain noted, "but how can I help?"

"There's a match coming up soon at Old Trafford between Surrey and Lancashire, and we think there is a good chance that it may involve a fix. Our plan is to stake out the pitch from the air. If the culprit does the dirty deed and rains, then we have a chance."

"But you can't apprehend a Cloud Machine in the sky."

"That's so, but we can tail it to its cloud lair and then call in our reinforcements on the ground to nab the blighter as it lands."

"Cunning! So, what do you want me to do?"

"We want to put a Police Constable on board your machine as an observer, and then you take up position and wait."

"Well, that's simple enough. When do we start?"

A couple of days later, PC Plod boarded the *Nimbus* at Wythenshawe in the early evening, and Puffy took him through all the various safety briefs. As soon as it was dark, the *Nimbus* ascended into the night sky and headed nowhere initially. The crew had already gone through the process of taking on board water with a hose pipe and immediately freezing it to store in the machine's refrigerators. Once in the night sky, the sublimators were switched on to convert the ice into a cloud that, when dispensed through the various vents around the fuselage, created a cloud that hid the *Nimbus* from human view.

PC Plod was amazed at the way things were done aboard the *Nimbus*. This was his first experience on board a Cloud Machine; in fact he didn't even know that they had existed before this assignment.

The next phase of the mission took the *Nimbus* the short distance from Wythenshawe Weather Centre to a position just north of Old Trafford Cricket Ground. This spot would enable the crew to spot any cloud travelling from the west on the prevailing wind that had any inclination to precipitate on the match, because it would have to cross in front of them from right to left. Now it was a case of wait and see, with liberal doses of coffee and bacon butties to help pass the time—another source of amazement for the resident policeman.

The crew of the *Nimbus* and PC Plod waited patiently for several days to see something suspicious, and they got quite caught up in what appeared to be a fairly evenly matched game. It was only in the final day that it looked as if things were going in the favour of Lancashire.

"Something will happen today, I'm sure of it," said the constable.

It was a grey day with wall to wall stratus clouds at five thousand feet, and a considerable number of Cumberland Greys went through on the wind at about three thousand feet. It was difficult to pick out individual clouds in these conditions, which was a bit frustrating. Sure enough, just as Lancashire turned the heat on Surrey to bring the match to a conclusion, it started to pour down.

"Which one is it?" asked Puffy.

"I can't tell in these conditions," replied the captain.

Cirrus moved the throttles, and the *Nimbus* moved forward, going straight through some of the clouds in their way, but that was of no consequence. A left turn put them behind the rain, but it was not coming from the cloud directly in front of them; it appeared to be from a cloud further ahead. The PC urged the captain to put on a head of steam. In spite of an increase in speed, the *Nimbus* had to travel through at least one cloud in front to reach the match fixer, but by the time they emerged from it, it had stopped raining.

"What do we do now, Constable?" asked the captain.

"Which one of this lot do you think it could be?" asked the PC.

"Look for yourself. We are surrounded by Cumberland Greys; it could be any one of them. I suggest we pretend to be one of nature's productions and just go with the flow. If the culprit is amongst this lot, then at some point it's going to want go somewhere that nature doesn't want it to, and we will spot it."

"Good thinking, Captain. I agree."

For a couple of hours the crew intently studied the TV screen on the flight deck, looking for abnormal cloud movement as they glided along on the current of air.

Nothing unusual was observed, and it was getting boring. *When you have seen one Cumberland Grey, you have seen them all,* thought the captain.

"Captain, Captain, thar she blows!" exclaimed Puffy.

"Good spotting, Puffy." As the three of them peered at the TV screen, one Cumberland Grey could be seen ascending, whereas all the others remained at the same altitude. "Let's wait awhile before we conclude that it is definitely the one we're after."

"Aye aye, Captain."

It didn't take the three of them long to agree that this was their cloud. "Captain, chase that cloud!" exclaimed PC Plod.

The *Nimbus* ascended in pursuit of nature's breakaway but was gaining on it very slowly.

"Give us more speed, Captain!" shouted the PC.

"I can't. I can't exceed thirty knots. If I do, I will be in breach of the *Cloud Machine Operators Rules*, and I will be in serious trouble," replied Cirrus.

"You're on Police business now, so crack on."

With the throttles wide open, the *Nimbus* started to gain ground in a more expeditious manner, but it looked as if the cloud in front was going to reach the stratus up ahead—and when it did that would be the end of things. That's exactly what happened. Once inside the stratus, there was no way the *Nimbus* could pick anything out in it, and so it stayed at a lower level just in case the escapee decided to descend into clearer air. After an hour the crew had to admit that they had lost it and it was time to go home. They assumed that the westerly wind had blown them over Yorkshire, but not knowing exactly where they were was not a problem; all they had to do was punch the latitude and longitude of Wythenshawe into the soakometer, and the *Nimbus* would find its own way back.

The Chief Constable of the Greater Manchester Police was waiting to greet the *Nimbus* on its return, but on discovery that the crew had lost the match-fixer, the greeting became decidedly frosty. "Damn it, we are back to square one!" exclaimed the chief constable.

A Tip-off

Mr Spite held an inquest into the recent cloud chase to try and establish if things could have been done any differently. "Cirrus, did you check to see if the match-fixer was using his ID beacon?" Every Cloud Machine had an ID beacon that transmitted a unique signal and indicated which machine it was. Its position relative to the receiving machine would show up on a plan position indicator. This was essential when visibility was zero, in order to avoid a collision.

"Yes, I did. There was no evidence that he was."

"That's unfortunate," said Mr Spite. "I suppose that the whole exercise will have to be repeated." And that's where things were left.

A couple of weeks later, there was an interesting development. Mr Spite had a call from a friend who lived in Silloth and had some interesting information. For several months a Cloud Machine had been operating from the old airfield and living in a house that overlooked it, nothing happened there that the man was not aware of. This friend knew what Mr Spite was involved with, and he knew that Cloud Machines were generally kept at Wythenshawe unless a special kind of job was being done. He clearly remembered the training that had occurred for the Great Cloud Parade and was interested to find out what was going on now.

A long conversation between Mr Spite and his friend in Silloth established the dates on which the Cloud Machine departed and returned from the airfield, and when these were checked against the dates of the abandoned games, they clearly matched. His friend could not give any information about the Cloud Machine's crew, where they were staying, or where they bought their provisions or fuel, but it was still an interesting development.

Mr Spite held a meeting with the Chief Constable to bring him up to speed with the latest information and to discuss the next move.

"Now look here, Mr Spite, we need to work out the next likely move that the match fixer will make," said the Chief Constable.

Careful consideration of the county fixtures list pinpointed a key match between Surrey and Derbyshire in just over a week's time, and there was general agreement that this would probably be the next target.

"We need to catch the crew as they are getting ready to depart."

"But you won't have any evidence," remarked Mr Spite.

"We already have enough evidence to pull them in for questioning. They have a lot of explaining to do as to where they have been and what they were doing on the dates the abandoned matches took place."

Discussion then turned to strategy. The group made a decision to place the *Nimbus* in a position where it could keep a close surveillance on the old airfield; a hit team would be on standby locally to intercept the machine before it could get airborne, when signalled to do so. They worked out dates and times and prepared an operation order.

In due course the *Nimbus* got airborne from Wythenshawe, and PC Plod was part of the surveillance crew once more. They punched the lat and long that had been given to them in the operation order into the soakometer, and the *Nimbus* headed north. The hit team had a grid reference to head for, and that was where they would park up and wait.

The *Nimbus* took up its position just to the north of Silloth Airfield and had a perfect view on the cockpit TV screen of the whole airfield. They radioed the hit team to establish that everyone was in place. After several hours, the crew observed a car driving through the entrance of the airfield and past the old airfield guardhouse before making its way to a position behind one of the big hangers on the main site.

"It shouldn't be long now," said Cirrus.

But the *Nimbus* waited and waited, and nothing happened. They had been expecting the hangar doors to open and the Cloud Machine to emerge to carry out some checks before getting airborne.

"What happens now, Cirrus?" asked the Police Constable.

"It's Captain to you Constable and wait and see."

"Beg your pardon, Captain."

The *Nimbus* hovered silently in the same position for another twenty-four hours, which was not too bad for the crew because they had ample food on board and a galley in which to cook, not to mention a toilet and a drop-down bunk in which they could take turns sleeping. The same could not be said for the hit team cramped inside a minibus. They had a very uncomfortable night but did manage to get some food from a local café, and they paid several visits to the local WC.

The following evening was graced with a full moon, which gave an eerie light to the old airfield, and Puffy fully expected to see ghost planes coming and going. It wasn't long before the doors of a large hangar started to open. A call to the hit team told them to standby; it looked as if this was it. The nose of a Cloud Machine started to slowly emerge from the hangar.

"Hit team go, go, go!" shouted PC Plod over the radio.

The crew of the *Nimbus* waited to see the minibus arrive on the scene and disgorge the policemen that would surround it and apprehend the match fixers, but it never came.

"Where on earth is that hit team?" remarked the captain.

The errant Cloud Machine was clearly going to get airborne any minute when a call came in from the missing squad. "There's nothing here, Captain!"

"What do you mean, there is nothing here? I'm looking at it now, and if you are not here in seconds, it will be airborne."

"Well, I'm telling you there is nothing here."

In total frustration the *Nimbus* watched the Cloud Machine lift off into the night sky and then disappear over the Solway Firth, presumably to atomise water that would be used later over a cricket match in Derby.

The *Nimbus* crew held a quick conference via the radio with the hit team, which was now more of a miss team.

"Now, just give me the grid references of your position," instructed the captain.

Puffy produced an ordnance survey map of the area, and by using the grid references given to him, he placed them at Kirkbride Airfield, which was a few miles to the east of Silloth Airfield.

"Bloody hell!" ranted the captain. "You are at the wrong bloody airfield. You're at Kirkbride, not Silloth. No wonder you didn't damn well see anything."

"We used the grid reference given to us in the operation order, so it's not our fault," retorted the equally frustrated hit team.

"What did you say happened?" replied Mr Spite, having listened on the telephone to the captain of the *Nimbus.*

The operation order given to both the *Nimbus* and the hit team was carefully scrutinised, and it became embarrassingly clear that it had sent them to two unrelated places. The confusion was down to the Police Authorities, which was a great relief to Mr Spite. The question now was what to do next.

The *Nimbus* received an order to remain in position until the match fixer returned, and the hit team would take up a new position in order that they could swoop on Silloth Airfield and not Kirkbride.

With new instructions in place, the *Nimbus*, having rained over Solway Firth to lose its cloud, sneakily landed at Silloth and anchored down for the night. The crew joined the hit team for a clandestine night out in Silloth's pubs. They all took a chance that the baddies would not return overnight, and their luck held out better than they did after a heavy night.

It was another forty-eight hours before anything else happened, but on an evening with a fair amount of natural cloud cover, it was not easy to spot any particular one. A bit of a break in the clouds allowed Cirrus to spot a short deluge over Solway Firth, and he had an inclination that it just might be the returning culprit dispensing with his anonymity before coming back to Silloth.

"Standby, everybody, this might be it!"

The captain screwed his eyes to try and pick out the naked Cloud Machine as it approached the old airfield in the dark. It was just as it descended towards the apron outside the hangar that he caught a glimpse of it.

"Hit team, go, but let the crew get out before making an arrest," shouted Cirrus excitedly over the radio.

"Gotcha, Captain," came back the reply.

The hit team's minibus could be seen hurtling around the old airfield before coming to a sudden halt behind one of the four big hangars. The Cloud Machine landed, and after a short interval the side door opened and the exit steps extended down.

"Hit team, they are about to get out!"

The minibus moved around to the front of the hangar, and the squad disgorged in record time to surround the two-man crew who had just disembarked.

"We've done it!" shouted a jubilant Captain Cumulus.

Mr Spite said, "Well done, Cirrus, and for that matter well done, Puffy and PC Plod. You have all done a sterling job."

"Can you tell us who the match fixers are?" asked Cirrus.

"Yes it's out in the open now, it was Bill Jones and his brother Ben, in the *Skylark*."

"Bill and Ben the rain men. I would never have thought it possible," remarked Puffy.

"Do you know who was behind it, Mr Spite?" asked Cirrus.

"That's for the court to decide, but you will find out—you and Puffy will have to be there. But for the moment, well done to you all once again."

Crown Court

At the Crown Court in Manchester, the charges were read out for the six men on trial for conspiracy and fraud. "Charles Dundee, Ben Wallabaloo, Michael Williams, and Andrew Sleuth, you are hereby charged with conspiring to fraudulently obtain money by virtue of taking bets on county cricket matches whose results you had fraudulently organised in advance. William Jones and Ben Jones, you are charged as accessories to the aforementioned by supplying the means by which the results of these matches could be fixed."

The first four charged turned out to be four Australians who lived in London and ran a chain of betting shops around the UK under the name of Betalot Winalot. The scam they had cleverly organised had netted them a very large sum of money, and not always by getting their punters to bet on a winner—they also got them to bet on which matches would get abandoned.

Bill and Ben both liked a flutter but simply did not know when to stop, and they got themselves into deep debt with the Betalot Winalot chain. The four Australians, having learned that the two Joneses had a Cloud Machine that could perform a multitude of tasks, saw this as a golden opportunity to put into practice a scheme they had dreamt up some time ago. Their lack of a means to an end had put the plan on the back burner until the solution was presented to them on a Jones plate. The hapless Jones brothers had got nothing out of it at all—they had simply been blackmailed into doing it.

Cirrus Cumulus, his engineer Percival White, and Police Constable Wilberforce Plod gave evidence, each of them providing a vivid description of their part in apprehending the defendants. The judge commended them for their contribution, which he described as being in the finest tradition of the British Weather and Meteorology Office. None of them fully understood this, but it sounded good.

The jury had little difficulty in finding all six defendants guilty of the charges put before them, and it was left to the judge to pass sentence. "Charles Dundee, Ben Wallabaloo, Michael Williams, and Andrew Sleuth you have all been found guilty by this court to the charges put before you. You have together set out to deceive deliberately those individuals placing bets in your chain of betting shops, and you have thereby falsely taken their money to satisfy your own collective greed. This court sentences all four of you to be interned in Her Majesty's Prisons for a period of four years."

One member of the jury could be very happy with that verdict, because that was what he had bet would happen at his local betting shop.

The judge went on. "William Jones and Ben Jones, you have both been found guilty by this court of acting as accessories by providing the means by which county cricket match results could be fixed. Before passing sentence, I have taken into consideration the fact that you were both coerced into this act as a direct result of your accumulated betting debts, and your sentence will reflect this. You are both sentenced to twelve months community service, and I am recommending that your Cloud Machine be quarantined during that period."

Both Bill and Ben were greatly relieved that they had not been sent down to prison, but they still had to find out what form their community service would take. They did not have long to wait. The solicitor acting on their behalf communicated the details to them by letter.

To Mr William Jones and Mr Ben Jones, Esq.

Community Service on behalf of HMG

> You are both to report for community service to Poulton-le-Fylde Sewerage Works at a date and time that you will be notified of in due course. The Poulton-le-Fylde sewerage plant is not automated and relies entirely on manual input for its successful operation. You will have a full part to play.
>
> You have both been assigned to the aroma elimination department, which is headed by Mr I. Broom, who will be expecting you. You are to be advised that a face mask is essential, and you must take steps to obtain one in advance that fits tightly.
>
> Your service will last for twelve full months from the date of your first attendance.
>
> Signed: G. Brown, solicitor

The Aftermath

Back in Slaidburn in the Cumulus home, Cirrus was sitting in his favourite chair with a mid-morning cup of coffee and a copy of the Daily Gloom. Puffy hung around the lounge door and waited for the reaction of his captain.

The headline on the front page stood out in stark black letters.

Cricket Match Fixing Four Head for a Spell of Fixed Gaol

Then followed the full story, which included a glowing report on the part played by a certain Captain Cirrus Cumulus and his engineer, Percival White, aided by Police Constable Wilberforce Plod.

"Puffy, Puffy, come and read this. It's fantastic!"

What a change, thought Puffy. *This is a really great day and one to be remembered.*

"Is that the letter box I just heard?" asked Cirrus.

"I'll just take a look, Captain."

Puffy returned with a large envelope which both men recognised as coming from the Guild of Cloud Owners. It was the latest edition of the *Monthly Downpour.*

Once the newspaper had been read, Cirrus opened the big envelope and scanned through the monthly journal. When he got to the awards section, he let out a cry. "Puffy, come and see this!" Puffy did so at a rapid pace because there was clearly a sense of urgency in his captain's voice.

Puffy was handed the *Monthly Downpour* opened at the awards section, and he read its contents hurriedly. There was a report on the actions of the *Nimbus* and its crew, and that was followed by the following announcement:

> In recognition of the gallant contribution in apprehending fraudsters recently, Captain Cirrus Cumulus, skipper of the Cloud Machine *Nimbus*, is awarded the Cloud Defence Medal and will hence forthwith be entitled to use the letters CDM behind his title.

In the same announcement it said:

> The engineer of the *Nimbus*, Mr Percival White, is recognised by being mentioned in Cloud Dispatches, which will appear on his record of service.

Mr Spite had not gone unnoticed, either, and the announcement included reference to him receiving a commendation.

This was a great day indeed, and one which Cirrus had long waited for. The icing on the cake came when he received a phone call from Abigail Windrush offering her sincere congratulations to both of them and expressing a wish to celebrate with them at their earliest convenience.

That night in Slaidburn was one to remember. The Hark to Bounty was as full to the brim as every pint glass, and well wishers and total strangers caught up in the pub festivities wholeheartedly toasted their village celebrities. "To Captain Cirrus Cumulus, CDM, and his faithful engineer mentioned in dispatches, Mr Percival White," was a toast that rang out more times than they could count. In fact, it rang out until they couldn't count at all!

THE GREAT SHINDIG

All Prepared

The idea of thanking the current inhabitants of the island of St Kilda for the way they had looked after Lucy Windrush after her crash landing had been on the back burner for some time, but it was not out of mind. St Kilda was actually the name given to a small group of islands to the west of the Hebrides. The one upon which Lucy had landed, and the only inhabited island of the group, was called Hirta, but most folk simply called it St Kilda. The only inhabitants these days were the fifteen military personnel who manned the radar stations.

Lucy had been most impressed by the warmth of the greeting she had received, but also by the sheer isolation of the posting. All the people she had met were so cheerful and clearly intended to make the best of their time in such a splendid but isolated location. She had felt a great urge to do something special in return for their hospitality, and out of this was borne the idea of the Great Shindig.

Lucy Pankhurst had agreed to compose a special piece of music for the occasion, and steps would be taken to get a top brass band to premiere the piece on St Kilda. After many laborious hours of contemplation and experiment, Lucy created a composition that would echo around Village Bay in a truly Scottish-sounding way, combining the shrill of pipes, the Highland fling, and the reel; the combination would make good use of the unique, rich sound and splendour of a brass band. When Leyland Band rehearsed the piece, those that were lucky to be present to hear it were enthralled and were compelled to tap their feet. Providing transport and accommodation could be arranged, the band was only too happy to visit

St Kilda. It was, however, the latter two issues which may be a stumbling block.

The Windrush version of Lucy got in touch with Flight Lieutenant Wally Waffler, the officer in charge on St Kilda, to let him know that from her end, everything was in place to have a Great Shindig. She inquired how things were at his end. Wally was delighted to hear from Lucy and had some brilliant news for her. After a lot of discussion with his team, it had been agreed that the erection of a large enough marquee for a concert was not really practical, and further, it was not practical to try and accommodate a full brass band together with the descendants of the islanders that had left in 1930. A solution had eluded everyone for some time until someone came up with the idea of using a cruise ship.

After considerable haggling at a high level, they had reached an agreement with one of the cruise line companies. Wally made arrangements for a cruise ship to call in at Oban on the east coast of Scotland, and here Leyland Band, descendants of the island inhabitants, Lucy and Abigail Windrush, and Lucy Pankhurst would embark for the sea journey to St Kilda. On arrival in Village Bay, the Great Shindig would take place on board the ship whilst it was at anchor in this panoramic place. An open-air concert platform for the band to play on would be constructed over the pool. The military personnel would be invited to join the ship's passengers in order to enjoy a very unique occasion which was guaranteed to entertain everyone in a manner not normally seen on board these luxurious vessels.

Without any doubt Flt Lt Waffler and his team had done a splendid job. But it didn't stop at that! On the day after the concert, the ship would remain at anchor in the bay long enough to allow the descendants, along with the Windrush sisters and anyone else that wished, to visit the island. Refreshments would be made available in the Puff Inn, which was a part of the small military encampment. The journey back to Oban would begin during the evening.

Captain Cirrus Cumulus and his engineer, Puffy White, received an invitation to the Great Shindig. When they got wind of the plans, they decided to make a contribution to it. Through the help of Mr Spite and

Eddie Stormbart, a considerable number of Cloud Machine owners offered to help, and a plan evolved. The entourage of man-derived clouds headed for Silloth about a week before the big event in order to rehearse their own part in the proceedings, which was a secret kept from everyone.

The conductor and twenty-eight players of Leyland Band, along with a few officials, were delighted with the arrangements, and everyone was looking forward enormously to the big adventure. Lucy Pankhurst eagerly awaited the premiering of the new composition, whilst on St Kilda there was anticipation of the history-making epoch that was soon to bring the island a newfound fame. Even the fishing industry was taking a keen interest in the information they had been given.

Getting There

The cruise liner had left Southampton to journey to Norway, but Belfast and Oban were both on its itinerary. The scenery on the approach to Oban gained considerable interest from those on board. The liner entered the Firth of Lorn between the Isle of Mull and the Scottish mainland, and then it proceeded into the Sound of Kerrera to reach its destination. The ship made a magnificent spectacle, anchored as it was in full view of this attractive Scottish town.

The first to embark in Oban was a sizeable contingent of the media, which included radio and TV crews as well as newspaper reporters. Word had clearly got around that something unusual and special was about to happen. Next to embark was Leyland Band and a composer who very likely would become a celebrity in the near future: a certain lady called Lucy Pankhurst! Then came the Pipes and Drums of the Sutherland Highlanders. Passengers quickly realised that something was afoot. There had to be a reason why the outdoor pool had a stage erected over it—and that reason had just stepped aboard.

The media got itself organised to witness and report on the descendants of those last inhabitants of St Kilda, who were boarding a ship that would, in a very short time, be making a nostalgic cruise back to the island from which their forebears had departed in 1930. The liner's captain and his first officer made a point of greeting them as they embarked.

A very special greeting was also waiting for the arrival of Abigail Windrush and her sister, Lucy. The search and rescue of Lucy had been the catalyst for everything that was about to happen, and the press wanted every morsel of the story. Only a little publicity had previously been given about the Cloud Machine collision over the Atlantic, and the way Lucy had consequently arrived at St Kilda. The subsequent search and rescue operation, named Operation Windpower, had received scant coverage previously, but that was about to change.

Cameras flashed as photographers juggled for a good picture of the star of everything connected with this momentous event: Lucy Windrush. Men with microphones, recording equipment, and TV cameras fell over themselves to get close in and capture everything she said. The more upmarket TV programme makers had set up studios on board so that they could conduct upmarket interviews with this new personality. Lucy took it all in her stride, as if she had been doing this kind of thing her entire life, and she insisted that everyone else who came aboard at Oban got fair coverage, although in retrospect that should not really have extended to a Glaswegian window cleaner who was taking his mistress on a clandestine cruise. His wife had a surprise when she watched TV that night—and so did he when he got back from Norway!

Whilst a stage was erected on the stern of the liner over the open-air pool, the two bands rehearsed in the vessel's luxurious concert theatre. The departure for St Kilda would not be until the following morning, and it was essential for the bands to get together. They had both agreed on a programme in advance, and each had thoroughly rehearsed their own bit, but there would be some joint pieces, and they needed the resources of all the musicians to get it just right. Whilst many of the liner's passengers sought an evening's entertainment in Oban, the musicians rehearsed, drank, drank some more, and eventually hit the hammock. The following morning the liner departed early, but few early breakfasts were consumed.

Whilst everything was going on in Oban, Captain Cumulus performed his final practice flight with the numerous colleagues who had decided to join him. Silloth was a handy place to train. This Second World War airfield had a large number of huge empty hangars that could house many Cloud Machines. The airfield was no longer active; the last aircraft had departed in the 1960s, but much of the main site was still intact. A cemetery on the eastern side of the former RAF station was testimony to its wartime role, with a number of aircrew buried there. Silloth was on the side of the Solway Firth, which trainee aircrews during the war had nicknamed Hudson Bay on account of the number of Lockheed Hudson aircraft that had perished in it. Today however, the Solway provided the Cloud Machines with a huge source of water to atomise, in addition to being the location over which they would train each night with the help of waterborne observers. It had been a concentrated training period, but they had stuck to it, and Cirrus was most pleased with the standard they had reached. It was unfortunate that Black, Black & Blackemore's did not bring the contents for their mixers until halfway through the training programme, but when they did, the results were astounding. People holidaying in Silloth at this time got a real treat each evening if they took the trouble to walk to the promenade and look out at the night sky; the same could also be said of those who were at sea.

As the cruise liner departed Oban, the Cumulus-commanded fleet of Cloud Machines departed Silloth with a common destination: the island of St Kilda, or Hirta to be more correct.

St Kilda Beckons

For those who had arisen early enough onboard ship, the early morning vista as the vessel cast off and steered through the narrow gap between the mainland and the island of Kerrera was worth seeing. A turn to port brought the ship into the Firth of Lorn, and on a south-west heading it passed between Mull and Colonsay to make for the open sea and St Kilda.

As the morning progressed, the purpose of this visit became clear. The media began a series of interviews, which the ship's passengers had access to in one way or another. A fascinating picture began to emerge from the descendants of the last people to live on St Kilda. St Kilda was a name given to a group of five remote islands one hundred miles off the west coast of Scotland. Out of the five, only Hirta had been inhabited; the remaining four, Levenisha, Dun, Soay, and Boreray, were at nature's pleasure. The people of Hirta were known as St Kildans, and prior to 1851 some 180 of these Gaelic-speaking people had lived on the island and made a living from sheep herding, crafting, and fishing. After 1851 the population never exceeded 100, and the last 35 St Kildans had departed for the mainland in 1930, bringing to an end a whole way of life. To be able to share a nostalgic return with these descendants was considered a privilege by the ship's cruise passengers; it would provide them with considerable bragging rights when they got back home.

Of almost equal interest were the stories that Lucy and Abigail were about to relate to their interviewers. Passengers were enthralled to hear of the job Lucy had been involved in, taking foreign aid overseas in a huge cloud convoy. No one had any idea that such a thing was possible. Mitigating the effects of the polar caps melting by taking the excess water to where it was most needed was commendable in itself, but to be doing it with Cloud Machines was something listeners and viewers could not have imagined in their wildest dreams.

Then came the description of Lucy's mid-air collision that had left her at the mercy of the wind. She told how she found herself in her Cloud Machine, the *Softly Blows*, flying slowly and serenely on a south-westerly wind between the islands of Barra and Tiree on her way to Skye when she suddenly experienced a strong south-easterly wind which began to blow the *Softly Blows* out into the Atlantic. She realised that her ultimate fate would probably be an eventual ditching, but it was her great fortune to spot St Kilda, and she made a last-ditch effort to crash-land on the island. She had no idea that there was a small contingent of military personnel on Hirta. She was rescued from the damaged *Softly Blows,* taken to the military camp in Village Bay, and treated like a royal visitor who had dropped in for tea.

It was at this point that Lucy's sister, Abigail, was brought into the media studio. The ship's audience was already captivated by what they had heard so far, and they would not be disappointed by what Abigail would relate to them.

She began by describing how the news of her sister's mid-air collision had reached her. Abigail was fortunate enough to be taken aboard the *Nimbus* which was dispatched to a position between the islands of Barra and Tiree on a jet-propelled wind supplied by the Irish Sea wind farms off the Cumbria coast; that fact astonished the listeners.

Flight engineer, Puffy White, had worked out that the jet-propelled current of air that had blown the rescue team to where they where, may have blown Lucy off her original course. That genius bit of deduction had led the team to St Kilda, where they had spotted what they had been searching for on top of Mullach Sgar, close to one of the radar stations.

At this point, loud clapping broke out amongst the thousand or so cruise passengers who had been caught up in this amazing story.

Attention turned again now to Lucy, who explained that the welcome she had received from the small team of RAF radar people on the island was heart-warming, and that same greeting had been extended to her sister and the crew of the *Nimbus,* which had landed to collect her. The sheer isolation and beauty of Hirta had captivated Lucy, and her admiration for the personnel based there and what they did filled her with a great desire to do something special. That was why she was here. Lucy requested at this point that her composer friend, Lucy Pankhurst, be brought into the interview, and after her arrival the two of them described how Leyland Band would be performing a world premiere of a new composition called "St Kilda's Fling" later that evening in a concert that would be jointly conducted with the Pipes and Drums of the Sutherland Highlanders.

No cruise liner had ever had passengers onboard that were so motivated by the experience, and a great expectation electrified the whole ship as it made its way across a smooth sea and under a clear blue sky. Nature was surely shining on this exciting initiative, and the world was rapidly getting to know about it as hundreds of e-mails, texts, and phone calls reached out to every continent on the planet. Lucy Windrush could be well pleased with the outcome of her unfortunate mid-air collision, which was now the talk of the world.

In mid-afternoon, as the liner got nearer to its destination, the first image of St Kilda came into view. The islands of Hirta and Boreray to its right were the first to be seen, and in the skies beyond lay a layer of clouds that gave nothing away about their real identity or purpose. In one of the clouds sat Captain Cirrus Cumulus with his feet on the flight deck, having a drink of tea and watching events unfold on his TV screen. Beyond Hirta and perhaps lying under the leading edge of the cloud layer was the only island of the St Kilda group that would remain out of sight: Soay.

The liner started to slow down as it approached the rocky lunar outcrop of Levenisha, which marked the entrance to Village Bay. The vessel almost came to a stop and then turned about to prepare it for a stern-first entry that would place the bands on board at the forefront of the vessel's arrival. This action was also accompanied by a huge redeployment of passengers who were anxious to get the best viewpoint.

The Pipes and Drums of the Sutherland Highlanders, in full regalia, filed onto the special staging that had been arranged above the ship's pool, and they were followed by the Leyland Band wearing very smart white jackets. The presence of all these musicians was a clear signal to all to standby for something special.

As the cruise liner headed slowly astern towards the bay, more detail became obvious. On the port side was the headland of the island of Dun, a finger-like protrusion from the south-east corner of Hirta, which was quite spectacular. Passengers with binoculars could observe large numbers of gannets and puffins. St Kilda's sea cliffs are the highest in the UK and help to orchestrate that wonderful sound that the sea can make when it embraces a rocky shoreline with its multitude of cavernous embrasures.

As the shore of Village Bay became visible, the presence of buildings became evident. A model-like village was dwarfed by huge hills: Mullach Sgar on the left, which was where Lucy had crash-landed; Oiseval on the right; and domineering things in the centre was Broda Mor Coachaire. As the liner got closer in, the many fishing boats at anchor provided additional and unexpected interest for the passengers. Their presence had been by invitation from the officer in charge on Hirta, Flight Lieutenant Waffler, via the shipping office, and they had anchored on either side of the bay to mark a clear channel for the liner. The crews of these vessels cheered as the liner neared, and the passengers cheered and waved back.

The cruise liner proceeded very slowly stern first to its designated anchorage, which had been determined by Flt Lt Waffler on the advice he had received from the cruise liner company. The people on board got a good view of both the old and the new village. The new to the right was a mixture of both, being a collection of modern green military buildings surrounding the old St Kilda's church and school, with the old vicar's house nearby. Hirta Harbour, which was little more than a jetty, was also on this side of the bay. In the centre and standing further back was the old village, which was simply a row of old stone houses that spanned the width of the bay from left to right. Some houses on the right of the row still had roofs despite the fact that they had been built in 1860. Behind the houses and clearly observable on the sloping landscape were numerous stone mounds known as cleats, as well as a small graveyard.

When the ship's anchor dropped, a silence descended on the vessel until the Pipes and Drums of the Sutherland Highlanders, accompanied by Leyland Band, began to play "The Flower of Scotland". The opening bars of the music brought a sense of serenity to the occasion, and those making something of a homecoming shed the first tears. The emotion rapidly spread and was heightened by both the presence of the crews of the fishing vessels standing on the decks of their respective boats and the RAF personnel who had gathered on the foreshore to welcome their visitors.

When the Pipes and Drums had finished, the mood changed as Leyland Band struck up with a rendition of "Imperial Echoes", which acted as a superb announcement of the ship's arrival. Joviality returned to make this a joyous moment that was already stamping an indelible image on the memories of those present.

Three small boats pushed out from Hirta's harbour to bring the full military compliment across to the liner and they received the greatest applause possible on arrival. Onboard they assembled to be greeted by the ship's Captain and then by that special casualty—Lucy Windrush who, much to Flight Lieutenant Waffler's surprise and those of his RAF team, kissed and then embraced him to which there was loud cheering. Lucy had returned and was already making her mark.

The Great Shindig

In the early evening, two of the liner's lifeboats, one from the port side and one from the starboard, were lowered to collect the fishermen from the boats in the bay. The fishermen made a splendid sight as they boarded the ship for the evening's entertainment. The liner's captain had had reservations about bringing them on board, thinking that they would be in their working attire and smelling of fish, but he could not have been more wrong. Each fisherman was dressed in the regalia of the Scottish Clan to which they belonged, and their pride was on display for everyone to see. *How the devil have they achieved that on board those wee boats out there in the bay?* thought the captain. This was a rare occasion, and it would be celebrated in style.

The various decks from the pool level up were stepped back progressively to maximise the view of the lovely bikini-clad ladies that would normally frequent that place, but this evening those attractive females would be replaced by two talented collections of musicians, and it would be for the audience to decide if the exchange had been worthwhile. The evening's concert would be in two parts, and the first was about to begin. In full uniform, the Pipes and Drums of the Sutherland Highlanders made their way onto the stage and received a warm welcome from an audience seated on several decks that now looked like theatre balconies.

The Pipes and Drums set the scene, playing "March, Strathspey and Reel", a lively traditional Scottish sound which, in this open-air setting, made the hairs on the back of one's neck stand on end. The shrill of the pipes echoed around the arena of Village Bay, and eyes scanned the isolated scene to absorb every emotional morsel that the combination of pipes and sea and cliffs and hills could provide. Right now this was the best place in the world to be.

The Pipes and Drums left the stage to allow the players of Leyland Band to conclude the first half, and after such a grand start they had a hard act to follow. Many of the audience had a stereotypical view of the music brass bands played, but that was about to change. The first piece of the band's concert repertoire had been carefully chosen, and it opened with "O Magnum Mysterium", a wonderful piece of Nordic music that fitted into the scenario perfectly. The sheer beauty of this music carried around the bay and entered the hearts of all. There was a feeling that the heart had been released and was ascending to a higher place, carried on by the emotional sounds permeating the atmosphere. Minds and intellect were left behind by the experience, for which the only release was tears, and plenty of them. The end came with both a feeling of relief and enduring enrichment, which was celebrated with clapping and a dab of a handkerchief.

After an hour of great music by two great musical ensembles, the interval was a chance to recover from the emotional drain and share a dram or two before the pleasure of St Kilda got underway again. It was pretty obvious by this time that whatever came next, the concert was going to be a rousing success. By the time the interval was over, the light was beginning to fade, and the coloured lights erected on shore by the RAF created a colourful backdrop.

The second half began with both bands on stage, and they played a number they had rehearsed together the previous day, "Highland Cathedral". This tune got the audience back into its warm and appreciative mood. The bands played several more numbers before Lucy Pankhurst and Lucy Windrush were invited onto the stage. Lucy P. was asked to talk about her new composition that was about to get its world premiere by the Leyland Band, and then Lucy W. spoke to the audience, describing the reasons for this evening's celebrations. At the end of their speeches, they both received huge applause.

As the two ladies stepped down from the stage, the darkness of the new night was highlighted by a glow that appeared above the tops of the hills in the foreground that now looked like a silhouette. The darkness blotted out any sign of the village, save for the lights on the foreshore. As the band was about to start playing Lucy's new composition, an illuminated Cross of St Andrew emerged from the cover of the hilltops, and the audience was in awe. This was the contribution being made by the Cloud Machine owners led by Captain Cumulus. They had formed up earlier with the help of a fishing boat which, being underneath them, had helped them form correctly to the west of Hirta. The glowing flag of Scotland remained stationary in the night sky as a backdrop to the rest of the concert, and its arrival coincided with the first rendition of "St Kilda's Fling".

Lucy had intended that her new composition would be a celebration of life and the virtue of living it happily. It had a Scottish flavour throughout, and a reel, a jig, and a fling were carefully interwoven in brass, capitalising on the very unique sound that was the hallmark of this kind of musical ensemble. The end came all too soon, but judging by the applause, this was a piece with a future. Both ladies looked up at the sky, caressed the Cross of St Andrew in their hearts, and blew a kiss to the Cloud Machines gathered above them. They knew who were making it.

The end of the concert was approaching, and it came as a complete surprise when the fishermen and RAF team assembled in front of the stage to form a choir that was accompanied by Leyland Band. First they sang "All in the April Evening", which was particularly poignant because the last St Kildans had allegedly departed Hirta that month in 1930. The quality of the singing was so good that there could be no doubt they had rehearsed this beforehand, but no one had said a word. The island's descendants on board were most moved by this performance and stood and applauded at the end. The choir had one more piece to sing before the concert ended. It was called "Elizabethan Serenade", and it ended things on a high note, at which point the huge audience stood under the gaze of the crews in the St Andrew's Cross and gave applause that wafted across the bay and up the hills; more than likely it reached the Scottish mainland.

With the concert at an end, passengers and musicians joined together for a celebration that continued into the early hours to cement the memories of the Great Shindig, and Captain Cumulus and his colleagues retreated out of view behind the hills of Hirta.

The Following Day

The following morning the passengers woke to find that the fishing boats had left; they had a job to do, and hopefully fish were waiting to be caught. The descendants on board had an opportunity to go ashore and visit the homes of their ancestors. The graveyard, church, and school were centres of attraction for them, as well as the old vicar's house. It was, however, the old graveyard to which most gravitated. There were names to read and memories to rekindle.

Some of the cruise liner passengers also took the opportunity to step onto the island of Hirta and wonder at the way life used to be for those born and bred here in years gone by. There is a tendency to romanticise these kinds of places, but in reality it must have been a hard life living in such an isolated place, with no means of communication other than the odd boat calling from the mainland.

Lucy and Abigail Windrush came ashore along with their composer friend, Lucy Pankhurst, and they all received a warm welcome from the RAF. Flight Lieutenant Willy Waffler was more than delighted by the way the Great Shindig had gone, and he loved the new composition. Those personnel currently serving on the island had a story to tell that no one was going to believe, but telling it would be a must. The team had laid on a buffet in the Puff Inn for the three ladies, and they were joined by an appreciative collection of the descendants. All this St Kilda air gave everyone a keen appetite.

Before departing the island, the three ladies visited the church to pay witness to the RAF memorial inside which paid homage to those who had perished there in the Second World War. In June 1943 a Beaufighter aircraft had crashed on Hirta, and in June 1944 a Sunderland flying boat crashed; the crews of each had been killed. On Soay a Wellington bomber had crashed, but no one could be certain as to exactly which of two it could have been, or whether it had happened in September 1942 or February 1943. No matter—all those men who had died were the sons of somebody, and it was right that someone remembered them in this isolated place.

With everyone back on board, it was time to depart for Oban, where the St Kilda-bound passengers would disembark, allowing the cruise liner to continue its passage to Norway but leaving a temporary hole in the ship's spirit. In the late afternoon, as the ship's anchor was raised, Leyland Band played a final but sombre piece of celebratory music that fitted the occasion, "Nimrod (Enigma Variations)".

But the ship was not going to go back in a melancholy way, and the Pipes and Drums provided a Scottish uplift that returned the spirits to a more upbeat level. When everyone thought that the music had ended and the islands of St Kilda were becoming small outcrops on the horizon, a solo bagpiper played a finale, a lament called "Fingal's Weeping", and as he played the islands disappeared over the horizon, bringing the chapter to a fitting conclusion.

EPILOGUE

Time for Reflection

Several days later, back in the Slaidburn home of Captain Cirrus Cumulus, CDM, and his engineer, Percival "Puffy" White, the two men sat down in the lounge and had a cup of morning coffee. For a change the captain was not reading the Daily Gloom, and there was no conversation between either of them. Both had decided to delve into their now substantial memory enclaves to savour the most recent and enjoyable of events.

Cirrus was thinking to himself, *I wonder if the cruise line company will decide to revisit St Kilda?* That led to other thoughts, like, *Will there be another Aurora Cloudealis, and will the cloud dance, Stormbart's Slow Stomp, ever go public?* He also thought, *I wonder what the next job will be?* But all that could be put aside for the moment.

"Puffy, go and get that jug of Rob's tea from the cupboard in the kitchen, and two glasses, please."

Blimey, it's twenty-six years since the captain drank from that jug, thought Puffy. "Aye aye, Captain, coming straight up!"

ABOUT THE AUTHOR

Former further education lecturer and officer in both the Air and Sea Cadet Corps, **A.L.(Tony)Smith** is married and lives in the north-west of England in a former mining and mill town. When his head is not in the clouds, he builds model aircraft and helps a local brass band.

Author Tony Smith, on the left, and Sqn Ldr Steve Hamilton, RAF, about to go cloud hunting.

ILLUSTRATIONS

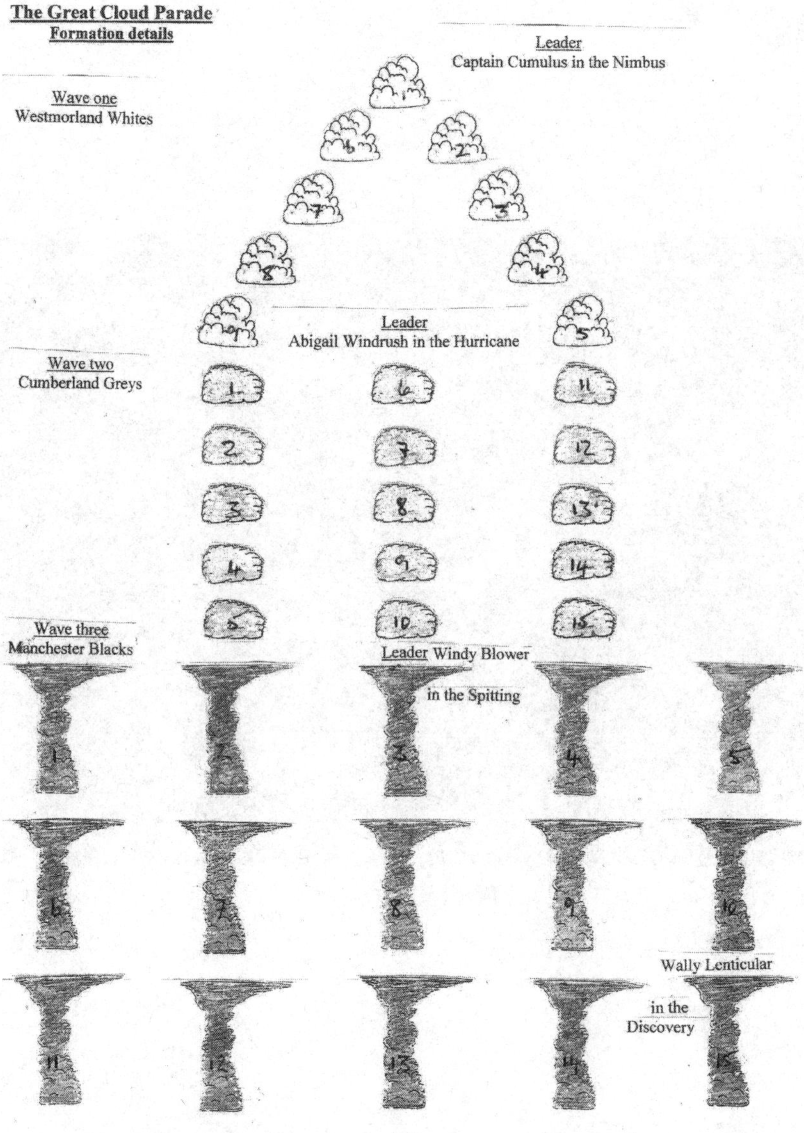

Formation details for the Great Cloud Parade

Hoghton Tower

Manufacturers – Black, Black & Blackemore's, Salford

Cloud Machine – Nimbus – grade 1

SIDE ELEVATION

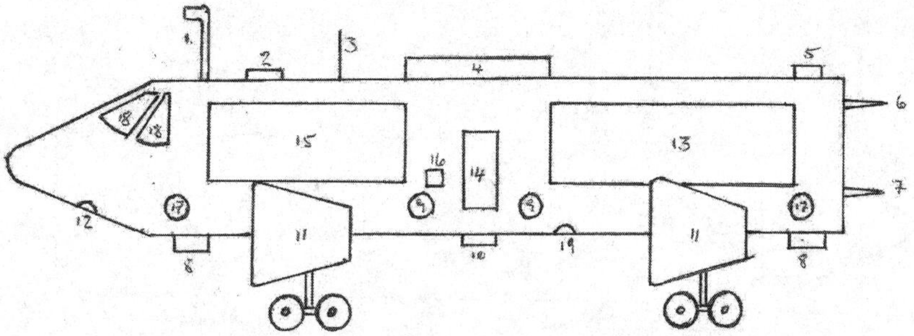

1. Periscope with tv camera which has infra-red capability to see through cloud or in the dark.
2. GPS antennae (Global Positioning System).
3. VSI antennae (Vertical Separation Indicator – used in cloud formation flying).
4. Emergency parachutes.
5. Identification Beacon (every cloud machine has its own ID code)
6. Telephone antennae.
7. Radio Transmitter/Receiver antennae.
8. Atomiser – converts water into cloud by a process of evaporation (some water is stored onboard, some as ice).
9. Dispenser – converts stored water and stored ice plus cloud vapour into rain by a process of melting and condensing.
10. SOAKometer – early form of navigation aid with built in water location system.
11. Fan Duct Motor – propels cloud. A cloud has its own natural buoyancy.
12. Porthole for winch cable.
13. Saddle type water storage tank.
14. Side entry door.
15. Fuel tank for Fan Duct Motors.
16. Panel of buttons to open/close entry door and deploy/retract entry ladders.
17. Loudpeakers.
18. Cockpit window.
19. Fuel hose point.

Side elevation of the *Nimbus*

Manufacturers – Black, Black & Blackemore's, Salford

Cloud Machine – Nimbus – grade 1

PLAN VIEW

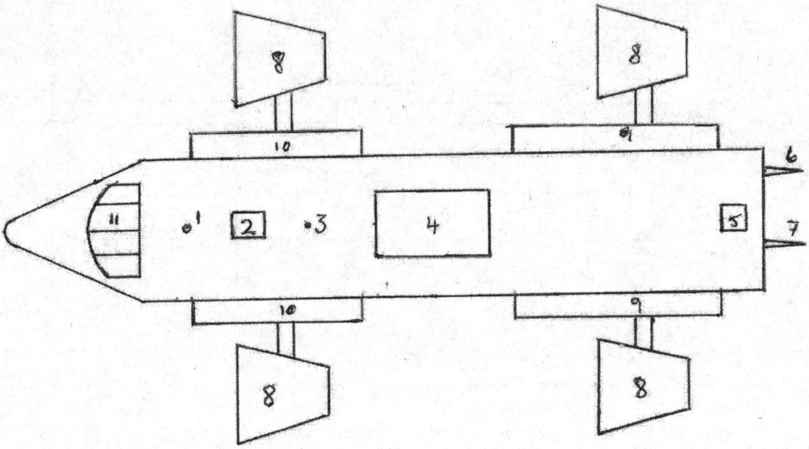

Direction of movement of Fan Duct Motors
to yaw the cloud left or right.
Movement made by cockpit rudder pedals.

1. Periscope with tv camera which has infra-red capability to see through cloud or in the dark.
2. GPS antennae (Global Positioning System).
3. VSI antennae (Vertical Separation Indicator – used in cloud formation flying).
4. Emergency parachutes.
5. Identification Beacon (every cloud machine has its own ID code)
6. Telephone antennae.
7. Radio Transmitter/Receiver antennae.
8. Fan Duct Motor – propels cloud. A cloud has its own natural buoyancy.
9. Saddle type water storage tank..
10. Fuel tank for Fan Duct Motors.
11. Cockpit window.

Plan view of the *Nimbus*

Manufacturers – Black, Black & Blackemore's, Salford

Cloud Machine – Nimbus – grade 1

FRONT VIEW

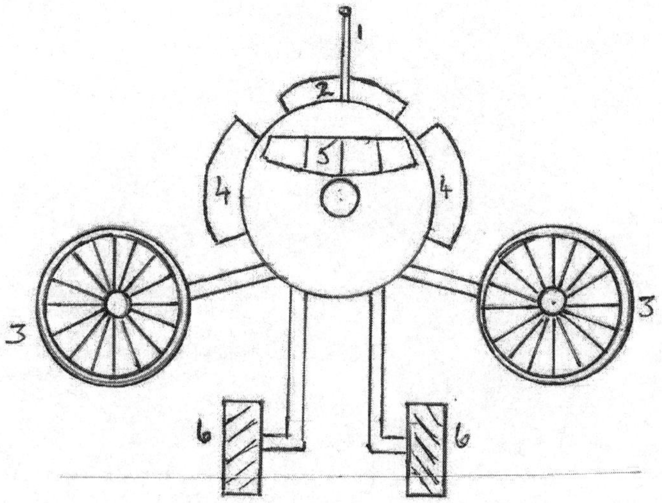

1. Periscope with tv camera which has infra-red capability to see through cloud or in the dark.
2. Emergency parachutes.
3. Fan Duct Motor – propels cloud. A cloud has its own natural buoyancy.
4. Fuel tank for Fan Duct Motors.
5. Cockpit window.
6. Rugged undercarriage.

Front view of the *Nimbus*

Manufacturers – Black, Black & Blackemore's, Salford

Cloud Machine – Nimbus – grade 1

GENERAL ARRANGEMENTS

Fan Duct Motors (port side shown)

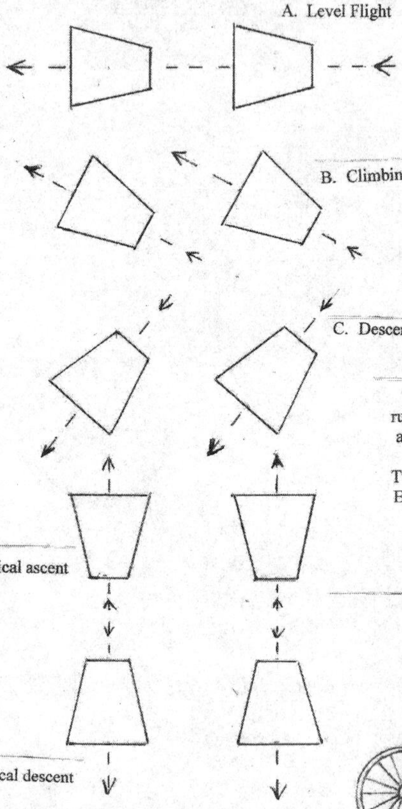

When a roll to port or starboard is required rudder pedals are operated to swivel the motors and the control column turned to throttle back the engines on one side of the craft. Turning (yawing) is achieved by swivelling the Engines but the craft skids without moving the Control column.

Note
Hovering is achieved by shutting down of motors or by going to position 'C' on a low setting.

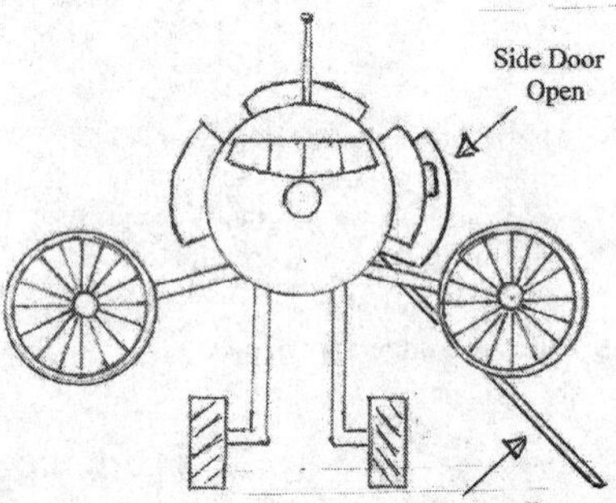

General arrangements

Manufacturers – Black, Black & Blackemore's, Salford

Cloud Machine – Nimbus – grade 1

INTERNAL LAYOUT

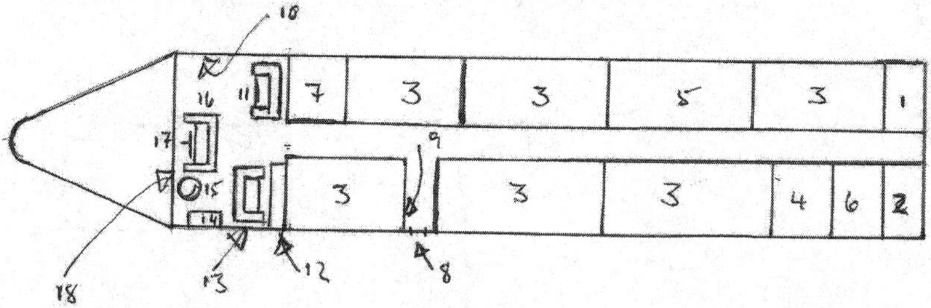

1. Wash room.
2. Toilet
3. Refrigerator.
4. Mixer.
5. Sublimator.
6. Van de Graaf Generator.
7. Galley.
8. Side entry door.
9. Panel of buttons.
10. Drop down bunk location.
11. Passenger seat.
12. Flight Engineer's station.
13. Flight engineer's seat.
14. Winch winding mechanism.
15. Plan Position Indicater.
16. Pilot's seat.
17. Control column.
18. Flight deck instrument panel.

Internal layout of the *Nimbus*

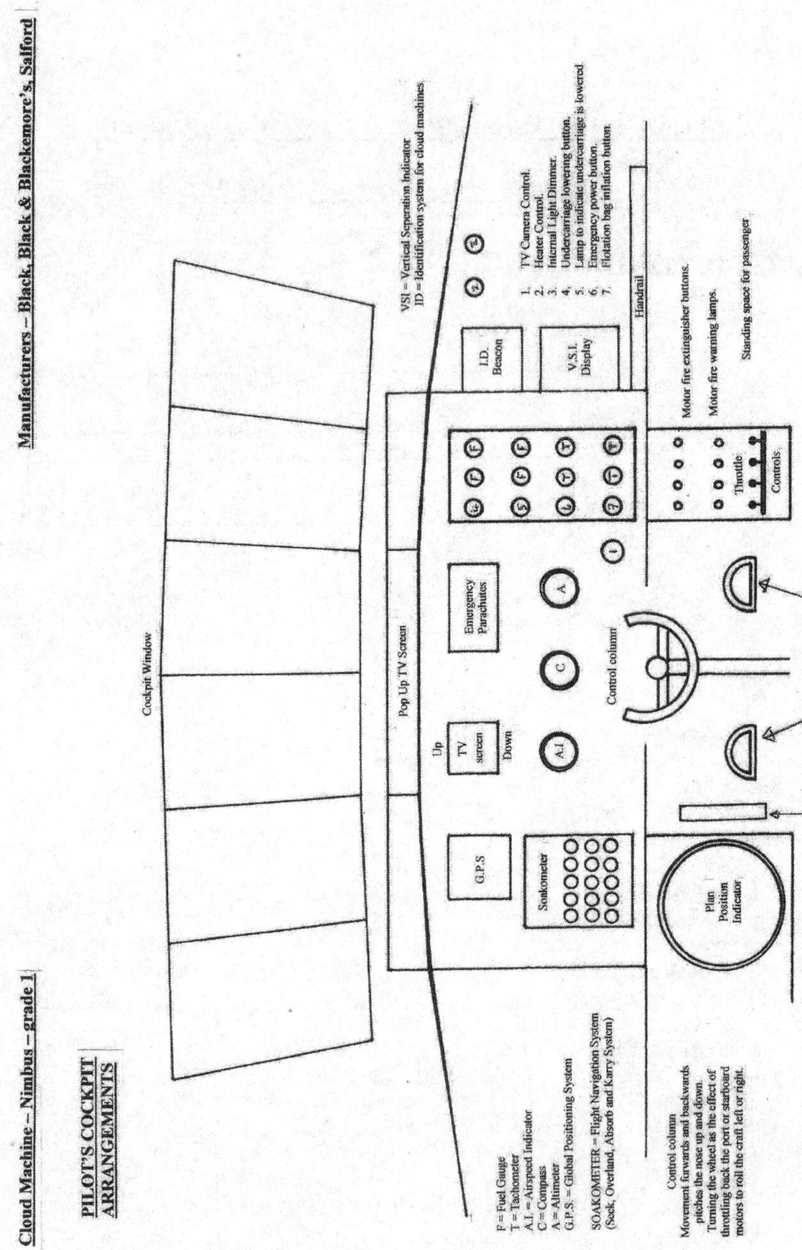

Pilot's cockpit aboard the *Nimbus*

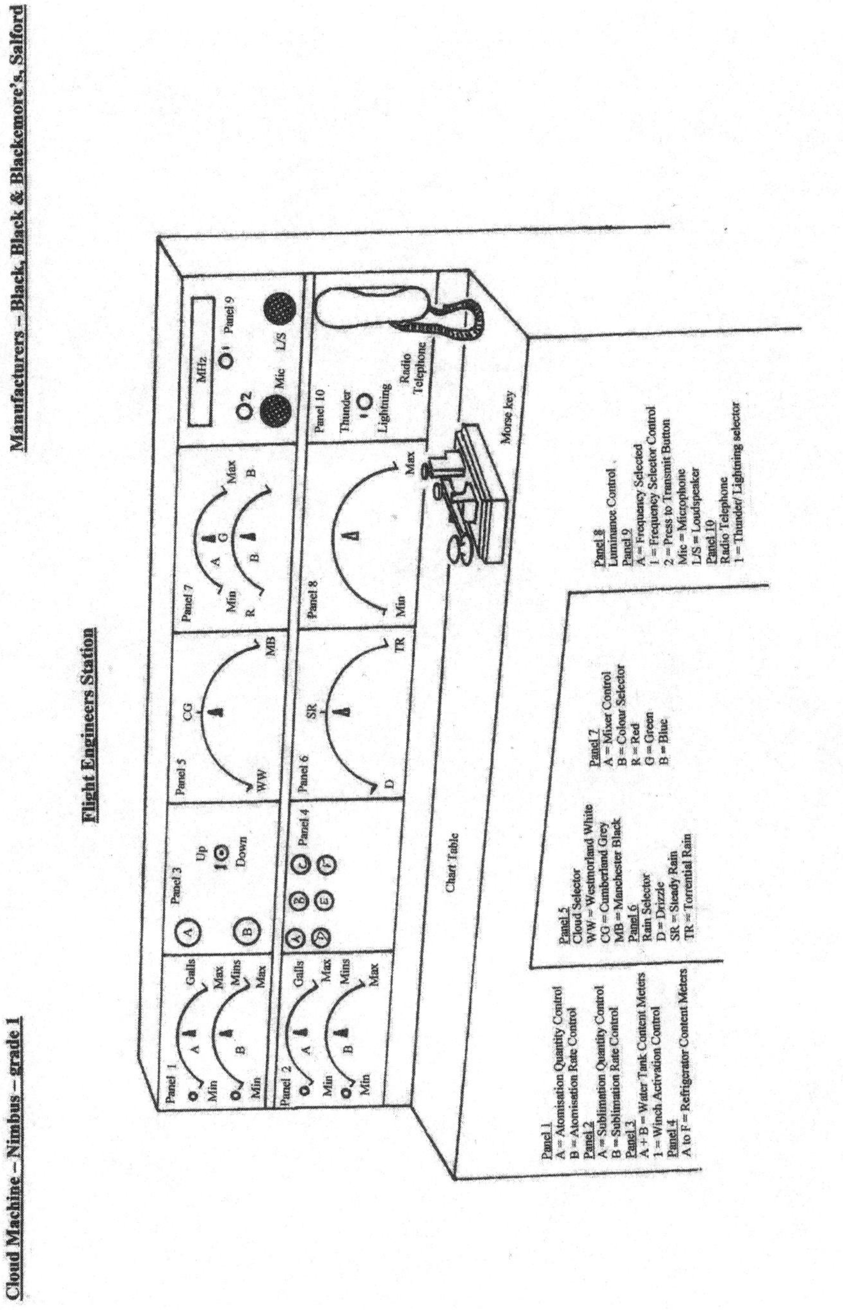

Flight engineer's station on board the *Nimbus*

MAPS

Flightpath of the Great Cloud Parade

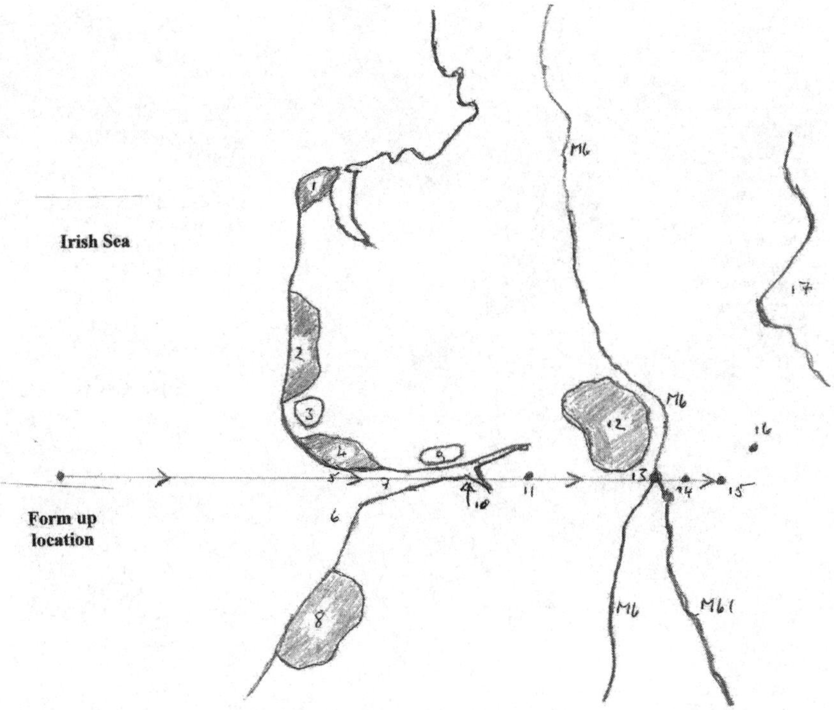

1. Fleetwood
2. Blackpool
3. Blackpool Airport
4. Lytham St.Anne's
5. Salter's Bank
6. Long Bank
7. River Ribble
8. Southport
9. Warton Aerodrome
10. River Douglas
11. Hutton
12. Preston
13. Junction 30
14. Gregson Lane
15. **Hoghton Tower**
16. Samlesbury Aerodrome
17. Bowland Hills

Flight path of the great Cloud Parade formation

Flightpath of search and rescue clouds

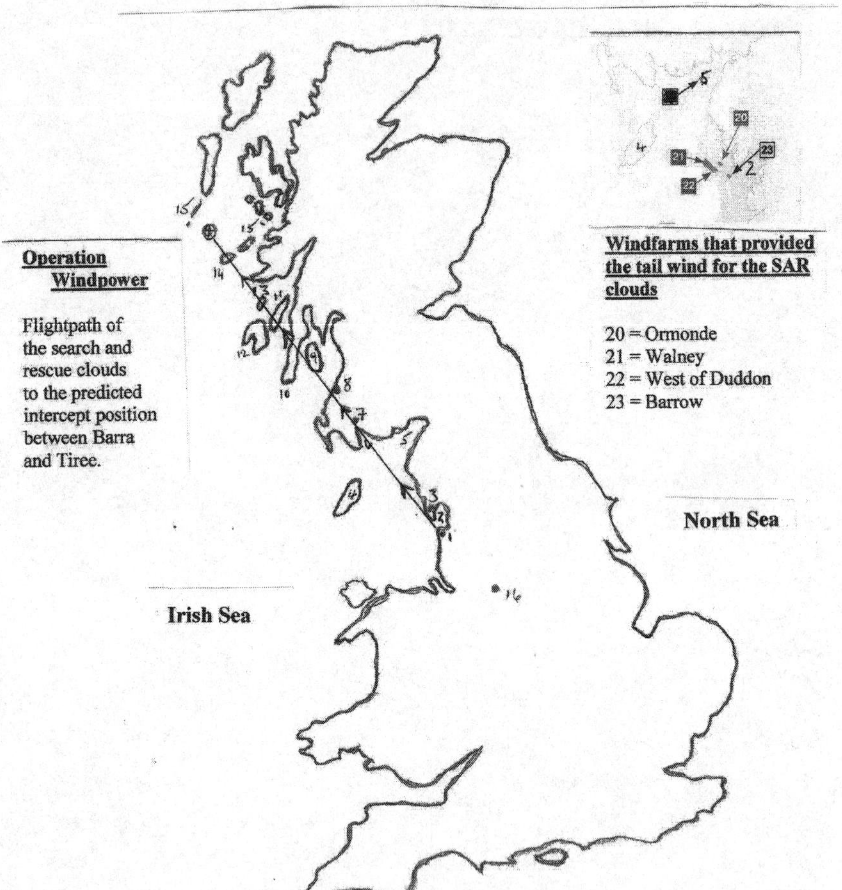

1. Fleetwood
2. Morcambe Bay
3. Barrow
4. Isle-of-Man
5. Solway Firth
6. Wigtown Bay
7. Newton Stewart
8. Maidens
9. Isle-of Arran
10. Mull-of-Kintyre
11. Jura
12. Islay
13. Colonsay
14. Mull
15. Coll
16. Wythenshawe

Flight path of the search and rescue clouds

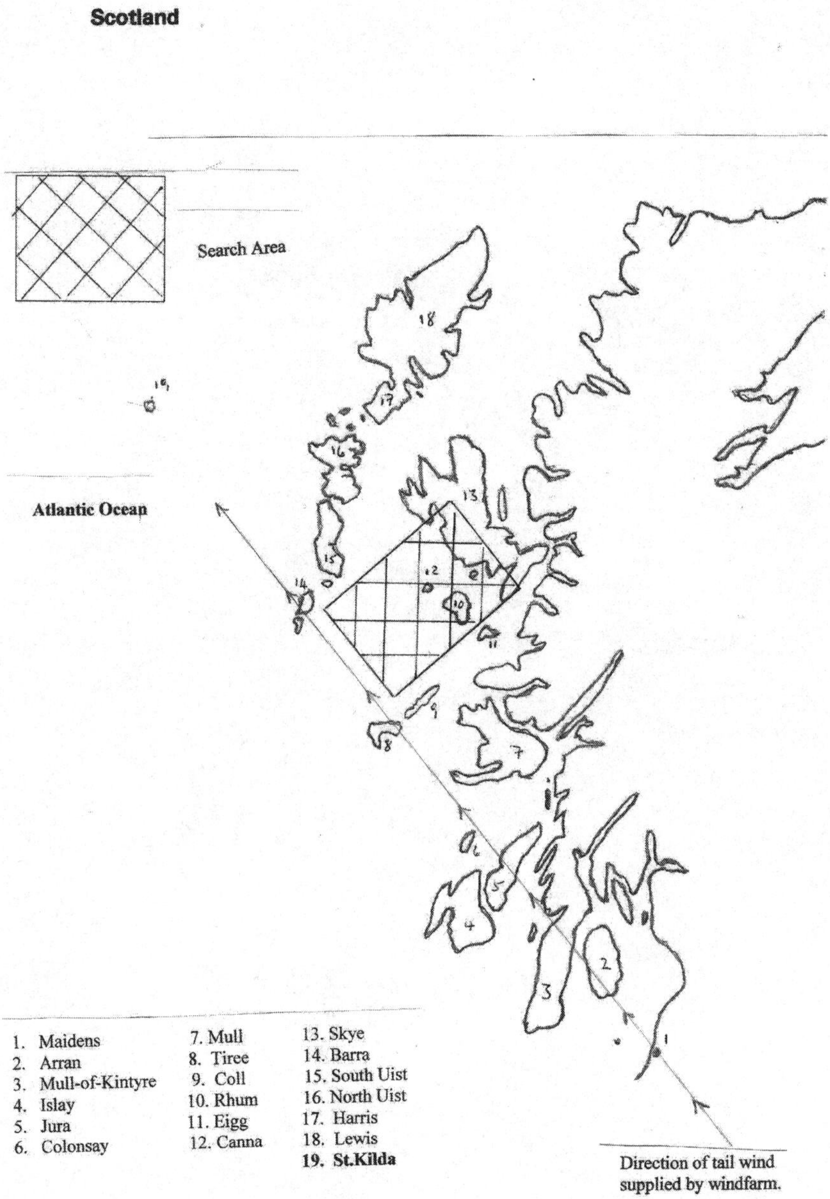

Scotland
Search Area
Atlantic Ocean
1. Maidens
2. Arran
3. Mull-of-Kintyre
4. Islay
5. Jura
6. Colonsay
7. Mull
8. Tiree
9. Coll
10. Rhum
11. Eigg
12. Canna
13. Skye
14. Barra
15. South Uist
16. North Uist
17. Harris
18. Lewis
19. St.Kilda
Direction of tail wind supplied by windfarm.

Search and rescue area

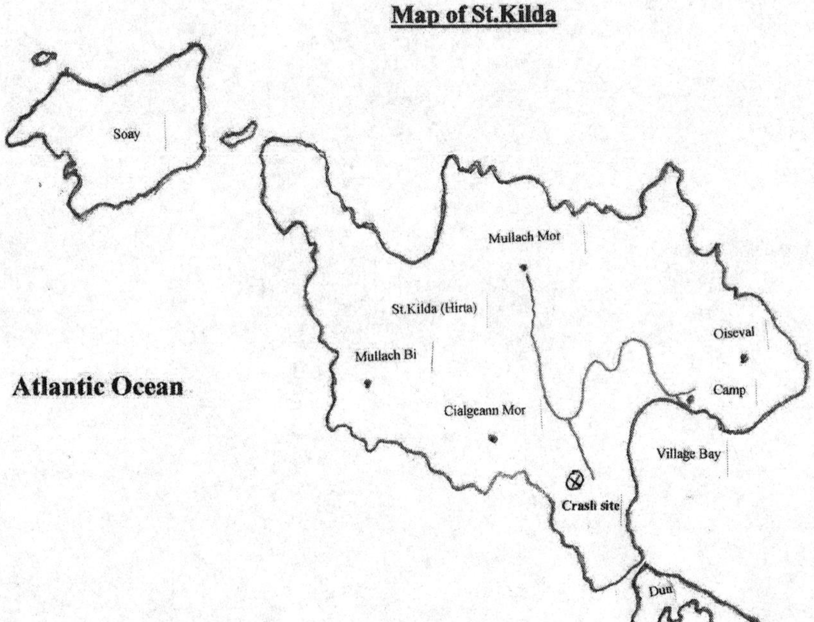

The island of St. Kilda